"Whether flipping burgers or speaking [...] *Work Worth Doing* provides humorous [...] age a paradigm shift—a new understan[...] God-ordained purpose."

SHAUNTI FELDHAHN,
bestselling author, social researcher, and international speaker

"Tens of millions of people have used Tom's apps and assessments to vie for jobs at the best companies in the world. Now America's #1 HR coach offers you the secrets for starting a purpose-filled career. Read and succeed!"

PAT WILLIAMS,
senior vice president of the NBA's Orlando Magic
and author of the bestselling book *The Success Intersection*

"The real reason we work is a secret no more! This book is packed with relevant insights. It's an absolute must-read and a crash course for Jesus followers entering the workforce or early in their careers. Tom shares what he has discovered by living it out. I've been the direct recipient of his wisdom as we worked together for more than 15 years."

GREGG DEDRICK,
cofounder of oGoLead, former president of KFC,
and chief people officer of YUM! Brands

"Written in an engagingly conversational style, *Work Worth Doing* is an invigorating antidote for anyone endeavoring to rise above the grousing and negativity of his or her work colleagues. Tom Heetderks provides a message designed to spiritually motivate and inspire."

REVEREND ROBERT SIRICO,
president, Acton Institute

"Tom writes in a way that gives us a fresh understanding of God's truth! Leaders today need these insights and wise stories. How good to know our work is an opportunity to worship God daily in big and small ways. Live this way, and you will hear the most important words of all, 'Well done, good and faithful servant.'"

CHERYL A. BACHELDER,
CEO, Popeyes Louisiana Kitchen Inc.
and author of *Dare to Serve*

"*Work Worth Doing* is smart, practical, and has an enormous heart. In a unique and highly engaging conversational style, Tom walks readers through a deeply personal encounter with the God-ordained purpose for what they'll spend their careers doing. Reading it made me feel as if I were having a heart-to-heart talk with a trusted mentor over a cup of coffee. Eminently accessible and brimming with spiritual insight, this book tells the truth and offers a path forward full of meaning and hope."

BRYAN DIK, PhD,
professor of psychology at Colorado State University,
cofounder of jobZology®, and coauthor of *Make Your Job a Calling*

"*Work Worth Doing* is an entertaining and inspirational book, and its deeply spiritual message will nourish any reader's soul. Tom has clearly and concisely articulated a transformative and motivational message that all jobs have intrinsic value with divinely inspired purpose. He inspires a desire to discover, pursue, and fulfill God's purpose for you in your work. Such a perspective will transform the heart and soul of any worker and give a new and higher calling to all."

ROBERT O. BUSE, MD,
neuroradiologist, medical director of the Department of Radiology,
and president of the medical staff of Baptist HealthCare

WORK WORTH DOING

TOM HEETDERKS

HARVEST HOUSE PUBLISHERS
EUGENE, OREGON

Cover design by Kevin Van der Leek Design Inc.

Interior design by KUHN Design Group

Work Worth Doing
Copyright © 2020 by Tom Heetderks
Published by Harvest House Publishers
Eugene, Oregon 97408
www.harvesthousepublishers.com

ISBN 978-0-7369-7926-9 (pbk)
ISBN 978-0-7369-7927-6 (eBook)

Library of Congress Cataloging-in-Publication Data

Names: Heetderks, Thomas D., author.
Title: Work worth doing / Tom Heetderks.
Description: Eugene, Oregon : Harvest House Publishers, [2020] | Includes
   bibliographical references.
Identifiers: LCCN 2019035471 (print) | LCCN 2019035472 (ebook) | ISBN
   9780736979269 (trade paperback) | ISBN 9780736979276 (ebook)
Subjects: LCSH: Vocation--Christianity. | Work--Religious
   aspects--Christianity.
Classification: LCC BV4740 .H4395 2020 (print) | LCC BV4740 (ebook) | DDC
   248.8/8--dc23
LC record available at https://lccn.loc.gov/2019035471
LC ebook record available at https://lccn.loc.gov/2019035472

Printed in the United States of America

20 21 22 23 24 25 26 27 28 / BP-SK / 10 9 8 7 6 5 4 3 2 1

*The LORD does not look at the things
people look at. People look at the outward
appearance, but the LORD looks at the heart.*

1 SAMUEL 16:7

Acknowledgments

Like any sound company or business policy, a book doesn't write itself. And for this book, I needed plenty of help and encouragement.

Thank you to the many people of the workplace, especially those who shared their stories and insights here. Gregg Dedrick, a leader during my younger days, thanks for helping me to "see it." Dave Neumann, a work friend of many years, thanks for providing the spark to get me going. Beth Claus, thank you for your many creative writing suggestions. And, David Sanford, thanks for sharing your invaluable guidance each step of the way. This book would not have happened without your prayers, patience, and amazing wisdom.

Dad and Mom, thank you for teaching me early on about God and work. Gwen, my loving wife, thanks for being my regular sounding board for many of the ideas in this book. And thanks to each of my three children, who provided the inspiration for me to put these words into print.

Most of all, thanks be to God. None of us ever work alone. With certainty, God will use anyone to accomplish His purposes—even someone broken like me. The crown-less craftsman of Nazareth who worked with warped and rocky materials so many years ago is the redeeming King who chooses to work with and through far-from-perfect sinners right now.

CONTENTS

FOREWORD

Tom Heetderks and I have worked together for more than 20 years, and few leading senior executives I have known have been more highly sought as a coach, supervisor, mentor, and work guide. More to the point, Tom has spent his career glorifying God at work through his approach and daily actions, living the words of this book.

I'm thrilled that he's created this gem. An amazing coach and mentor, Tom has helped countless others discover their unique talents and paths for glorifying God at work. As he points out, the book started to take shape as a fatherly love letter to his three children. It began from the heart and remains true to this love for others throughout. It's a remarkable accomplishment, and I'm excited for the current and future workforce that stands to benefit from reading and applying these powerful insights.

The message is this: God can use anyone, and He wants to use you. The power comes from the clarity of the message, and the challenge comes when readers take it to heart and work—deeply—to discover how God wants to use them in the workplace. *Work Worth Doing* will send them on a path filled with more purpose at work than they ever could have imagined!

After working as a psychologist and senior executive in the business world for more than 30 years, I can confidently state that this relatable book is for everyone—at any career stage. It is a great resource for students and those just entering the workforce, and it will go far in helping them launch their work experience in a positive, God-glorifying manner. Additionally, though, people of all ages and experience levels are looking for meaning in their work, and *Work Worth Doing* will also help them discover how God wants to use them in His vast workplace.

Dr. Dave Neumann, PhD,
Fortune 500 Executive

ABOUT THIS BOOK

As we waved, our older son drove to the street's end, beyond our limited view, and into his future. We wailed our loudest goodbyes. "We love you!"

In his discolored car, he had all of his few possessions, including fresh-out-of-the-oven brownies from his loving mom. He had just graduated from a nearby university and was on his way to start his first professional job in a Midwestern city far away.

"The days are long, but the years are certainly short," I said to my wife. And while we stood there, any further words of consolation fell faintly to the ground. I looked at her for a time, reflecting on our two decades as parents. I pondered our younger son, who at the time was a college sophomore, and our daughter, who was a high school senior, and then a few hours later, I penned a fatherly love letter to our children.

This book grew out of that short letter. If you're trying to figure out what to do with your life, this book was written for you—especially if you're a student or early into your career. But I hope to encourage any reader who's wondering about or struggling with work.

I'll help you answer common work questions and connect the dots between our God, the worthiness of what you do, and who you're meant to be. Here and there, I'll invite you to check out additional input in the Going Deeper section at the end of the book, which you can read either right then or later. I've also provided two self-assessment sections, as well as some insight for when you don't like your job and some tips for when you're looking for a job.

Last, throughout these pages, you'll see text that looks like this:

"This?"

Yes. Though we've not yet met, imagine this is a conversation between us. When you see a bolded subhead, it's as if you're asking a question or sharing your thoughts. Sound good?

"Yeah."

And why did I include so much Scripture? Because our many years spent in work are so much more than window dressing to the claims of our faith. They're core to our Christian living. Yet in *Work: A Kingdom Perspective on Labor*, professor of New Testament Ben Witherington III stated, "If you survey the topical indexes in works of biblical and systematic theology you will find the topic *work* rarely—because it is rarely discussed in the text of such books! How odd, especially when the Bible has so much to say about work, past, present, and future."[1]

Yes, the living and infallible Word of God (2 Timothy 3:16; 1 Thessalonians 2:13; Hebrews 4:12) has a *lot* to say about work! As president of Marketplace Leaders, Os Hillman tells us, "Work, in its different forms, is mentioned more than 800 times in the Bible—more than all the words used to express worship, music, praise, and singing combined."[2] And as author D.H. Jensen noted, "Biblical narratives overflow with work. Between the opening lines of Genesis, which portray God as a worker, and the closing chapter of Revelation, with a vision of new creation, God labors. One of the distinguishing characteristics of biblical faith is that God does not sit enthroned in heaven, removed from work and willing things into existence by divine fiat."[3]

To prepare your heart for this exploration of work, then, consider these Bible verses:

- "All Scripture is God-breathed and is useful for teaching, rebuking, correcting and training in righteousness" (2 Timothy 3:16).

- "We also thank God continually because, when you received the word of God, which you heard from us, you accepted it not as a human word, but as it actually is, the word of God, which is indeed at work in you who believe" (1 Thessalonians 2:13).

- "The word of God is alive and active. Sharper than any double-edged sword, it penetrates even to dividing soul and spirit, joints and marrow; it judges the thoughts and attitudes of the heart" (Hebrews 4:12).

Although in this book I'll assume you're a believer, you may be someone who says *no* or *never* to Jesus's teachings. That, however, doesn't mean you can completely bypass what He said about your talent, work, and service. And if you're inclined to refute the deity of Jesus, suggesting He was just a prophet or carpenter, note this: Jesus said, "All will honor the Son even as they honor the Father" (John 5:23 NASB). In addition, the Bible tells us Jesus "existed in the form of God" (Philippians 2:6 NASB), and a disciple addressed Jesus as God only to be praised by Jesus (John 20:28).

I also want to be clear about something else upfront. This book is about working, but it's about working *only* in the context of something far more important: your life and eternity. And no matter your place in life, you're there for a reason.

No matter your starting point—in faith and in the workplace—get ready to learn and prepare your heart for change. I promise to not only prod and challenge you, but also to encourage you along the way. Together, with an emphasis on the Bible's work-relevant accounts of King David's life, let's take on some of your lingering questions. And as we talk about you and your work, be reminded of God's love and power with every step. Almighty God is in control, and His Word says, "Blessed is the one who trusts in the LORD, whose confidence is in him" (Jeremiah 17:7).

My prayer is that, in this book, you'll discover a word, a verse, or a thought that convinces you that your work matters a whole lot more than you ever imagined.

GOD CAN USE ANYONE

It's disgusting to think about, really. The world of work received the touch of death thousands of years ago. It happened quickly, but it happened. You can read the entire, uncensored, 600-plus word account in Genesis 3, but here are a few of the most relevant verses for our discussion:

> Because you…have eaten of the tree of which I commanded you, "You shall not eat of it," cursed is the ground because of you; in pain you shall eat of it all the days of your life; thorns and thistles it shall bring forth for you; and you shall eat the plants of the field. By the sweat of your face you shall eat bread, til you return to the ground, for out of it you were taken; for you are dust, and to dust you shall return (verses 17-19 ESV).

This wasn't some cheesy martial arts movie, and the assassin didn't wear a topknot. No, according to Holy Scripture, a heartless, evil perpetrator in the form of a serpent wreaked havoc, and the world and the vast workplace in it was wrecked.

Now you're witness to the continued forceful attacks on an already beleaguered institution, and because of this, the workplace isn't for the faint of heart. It's just not.

I don't know how you got this book, but I will say you got it at a great time. That's because the earth and the workplace have both been waiting for you for a very long time!

"They have?"

Yes. And listen to this carefully: *God can use anyone, and He wants to use you.*

Can the preceding ten words be true? Read them again. Do you believe them—really believe them? Because there's no sorta or kinda-maybe here.

Some people find these ten words quaint; others find them laughable. That's because they either don't believe in God at all or have a distorted concept of Him. For many, a busy supreme being wouldn't help us see a new opportunity, call us to an exciting challenge, or use us for noteworthy impact. And sadly, unless it's to belittle someone's faith in "a sky daddy" or "little baby Jesus," a good many people are too stubborn, apathetic, or put off to even care how God might have anything to do with our work.

Know this up front, though: Although you'll never *grasp* everything about God, you can *trust* many things about Him. Our God is eternal, all-powerful, and all-knowing. Much more than the "old man upstairs," He's a distinct Holy Spirit who is near, active, and inescapable throughout our world. Nothing—and no one—compares to Him. And according to Him, those ten words—*God can use anyone, and He wants to use you*—are true!

Your Creator, who will reign forever, wants to do more through you than you can possibly conceive. In Scripture, we read, "[God is] able to do immeasurably more than all we ask or imagine, according to his power that is at work within us" (Ephesians 3:20).

"Okay. I hear you. You've given me a lot to think about already."

Good. Now let's look at King David, who's profiled at length in the Bible. For a Scripture review highlighting several parts of his life (and at least one interesting fact about another anointing), check out *A* under "Chapter 1: God Can Use Anyone" in the Going Deeper section of this book. But here, let's pick up the events when David was about 15 years old.

David is that peach-fuzzed teenager leaning against his staff over there by the hill who's "ruddy" and has "beautiful eyes and a handsome appearance" (1 Samuel 16:12 NASB). Right now, he's working as a shepherd for his family. But when he's not herding animals and doing pasture chores, David passes the time playing on his lyre and singing songs. He also messes around plenty with his slingshot, flinging stones at small targets.

For the most part, the rather forgettable, decidedly predictable days of his youth blend together. On any given hot-and-dusty day, he can be found doing pretty much the same old thing: herding sheep, slinging stones, and singing songs.

"That sounds pretty boring."

But soon there's a break in the story for David and his family. Their everyday house is packed with people—David's seven older brothers; their dad, Jesse; and Samuel, who's a judge, prophet, and religious leader. Samuel assumes the role of a high-pressure talent scout. And as he's done before, stunningly, he'll handpick the next king of Israel! This time, though, God limits his regal choice to a one-family candidate slate (1 Samuel 16:1).

"Sounds crazy."

Yeah. If this were a single-day vetting for a foremost country's throne today, the brothers would be pacing anxiously with quickened breath. Sick with anticipation, and on the cusp of untold fame, power, and wealth, they would also be dressed to impress, with faces shaved, shoes shined, and hair combed just right.

Okay, first brother up. Whoa. To his surprise, Samuel thinks he's identified the next king already. For him, Eliab is the obvious choice. He looks around, now openmouthed, and says, "Are you seeing what I'm seeing?" More literally, from the NIV translation of the Bible, "Surely the LORD's anointed stands here before the LORD" (1 Samuel 16:6).

Samuel is ready to declare, "You're hired!" But God says to him, "Do not consider his appearance or his height, for I have rejected him. The LORD does not look at the things people look at. People look at the outward appearance, but the LORD looks at the heart" (verse 7).

Rebuked from on high but somehow resolute to finish the task, Samuel proceeds to assess each of the remaining brothers. Disappointingly, though, as far as he can tell, the suitability of fraternal pickings seems slim to none. He utters something like, "Jesse, are these all your sons? Did all of your boys know I was coming today?"

Jesse admits he has another son but says he's basically the runt of the litter, not someone anyone with a sharp eye for talent needs to see. Essentially, it's as though he's saying, "Folks, move along. There's nothing to see here." After all, only one job—an entry-level job at that—is on this son's starter-kit résumé: boy shepherd.

As a last resort, Samuel requests to see this son anyway, and as David enters the scene, God declares to Samuel, "Rise and anoint him; this is the one" (verse 12).

David is more than dirty and smells like free-range sheep. (He also wouldn't have shaved because, well—how do I say this?—he didn't need to yet.) But as his passed-over siblings look on, their jaws hitting the dirt, their kid brother is anointed the next king of Israel.

Him? Our little brother! Are you serious?

Are you with me so far?

"Yes. God chose David even though he didn't seem like king material."

That's right. Here's a singular, priceless takeaway for you to treasure always, a spirited and affirming message I'll repeat many times in this book: No matter how improbable it seems, God can and will use anyone to accomplish His purposes.

Now let's go back to those ten words: *God can use anyone, and He wants to use you.*

When you read that, do you think your shortcomings are so unique that those words can't be true? Do you believe you're just too young or too inexperienced? Because if you do, I'd like you to remember a pregnant-out-of-wedlock teenage girl named Mary, who became the mother of Jesus.

If you're feeling too uncertain to believe those ten words, check out Jonah's and Joshua's stories in Scripture to see how God used them despite their initial misgivings.

Do you feel written off? Learn about a tax collector named Matthew, who became one of Jesus's disciples.

Are you unwanted? Recall that Joseph, who later became rich and powerful, was so undesired that his own brothers sold him into slavery. (You can find Scripture references for all these stories in *B* under "Chapter 1: God Can Use Anyone" in Going Deeper.)

Today, if God has anything to do with it (and He has to do with everything), a soon-to-be torchbearer somewhere in the world may be rather tired of life, drifting between *I don't know* and *I don't care.*

Perhaps that drifter looks a lot like you.

You might say, "God's not going to use someone like that!" Uh, are you sure? Because when He's not tapping a talking donkey to deliver a message (Numbers 22:28), just look at the seemingly weak, unlikely, and foolish individuals with far-from-perfect records He chooses and uses throughout His Word. It's an amazing pattern we see over and over again.

No one thought David would be "the one." But God said, "He's My choice!" Next to no one thought Peter, Rahab, Moses, Daniel, or Esther would be the one. And these days, few believe they're the one either.

"Why is that?"

Well, very often, we have a limited view of ourselves because we've bought into the deceits we've been told. Yet the Bible says God has a plan for each of us. You, for example. You've been preciously chosen, divinely anointed, strategically placed, and fully empowered to work with God. You're uniquely equipped for the good works He's prepared for you alone to do. Ephesians 2:10 says, "We are his workmanship, created in Christ Jesus for good works, which God prepared beforehand, that we should walk in them" (ESV).

Are you feeling limited? If you are, get ready to stop feeling that way. As God's awesome workmanship, never forget whose you are—forevermore.

"You're right. Feeling limited isn't great."

No, it isn't.

Back to David…

After being anointed king as part of the Lord's perfect plan, David returns to his shepherd role. That's right. After being chosen as his country's next ruler, he goes back to the grit and grime of herding sheep and slinging stones. And for several years that follow, he does pretty much this same thing.

Put yourself in his well-worn sandals. Can you imagine what he was thinking that whole time? What David was doing in the dirt must have felt to him like a long way from the throne; so to say the least, this had to be a puzzling time. (*Was the anointing a dream? Or was I punked by my father and brothers?*) It's a safe bet that this boy shepherd never imagined that, someday, he would be considered the greatest king of Israel, his kingship would be eternal through Jesus (2 Samuel 7:8-16, 29), and God would describe him as "a man after my own heart" (Acts 13:22).

But David was always working, and God was always working on David.

Most days, this would-be king still put a stone in his sling, swung the sling around his head, and jettisoned the stone toward a target. Once in a blue moon it was to kill a wild animal, but beyond that rare instance, this finely honed skill had about as much value as one-hand clapping, beatboxing on a unicycle, and— as much as I appreciate this one—artfully folding napkins into cute animal shapes. That is, not much (or so it seemed).

Later, Jesse calls David in from the fields and, in a father-son talk, informs him that a few of his brothers are involved in a battle. David isn't old enough to fight, but his father wants him to go to the front line and deliver food to his siblings.

Early the next morning, David leaves his flock in the care of another shepherd and sets out with a knapsack filled with cheese, cracked wheat, and bread. And then, in the storied Valley of Elah, he sees the armies from Philistia and Israel on opposite hills. A battle-tested, larger-than-life Philistine dominates this scene.

"*Goliath.*"

Yeah, Goliath is topped in a helmet and covered in a full-body, bronze-scale tunic. He has a javelin, a sword, and a short-range spear. And behind this intimidating killer and his revolting taunts, the Philistines are on the cusp of capturing the mountain ridge near Bethlehem and slicing King Saul's kingdom in two. The king and his Israelite army are terrified.

Among all gathered, however, is one Israelite who views this situation differently.

"*David.*"

David asks, "Who's this man who's allowed to talk this way?" And to the mouth-opening surprise of those gathered, he goes to King Saul, clarifies the financial incentive for winning the fight, and requests to battle the trash-talking adversary.

The king scoffs, "You're just a shepherd!" Even David's brother Eliab tries to disqualify him because of his lack of training. He jeers, "Why have you come down here? And with whom did you leave those few sheep in the wilderness?" (1 Samuel 17:28). Essentially, he tells David he's ill prepared and to go home.

Hmm. In a single Bible chapter, David is dissed by his powerful king and one of his own brothers.

"Why the disrespect?"

In the eyes of others, David is too young and inexperienced. As far as they're concerned, this impudent kid is removing the training wheels before he's earned the right to do so. And he's a shepherd—one of the least respected professions of the day.

Saul tells David he won't send him into battle. However, as is soon clear, the king has no alternative. And with a turn in the story, as a last resort, he equips the bright-eyed walk-on with armor.

Quickly, though, David sheds this needless covering, and our fledgling fighter grabs his leather-pouch sling. Then he proceeds, as he has for many years, to pick up a few stones. He's more than prepared. And you know where this (and one of the stones) is headed.

David not only believes those ten words—*God can use anyone, and He wants to use you*—but he adds an exclamation mark. He doesn't limit God or himself. And to the shock of all within earshot, he proclaims, "You come against me with sword and spear and javelin, but I come against you in the name of the LORD" (1 Samuel 17:45). Then, with his game face on, he runs at Goliath.

And the most-talked-about death match in 3,000 years begins.

Our young slinger sends a stone rocketing toward the too-big-to-miss target. This time, rather than a bear, lion, or imagined target, though, his bull's-eye is perhaps a pimple on a swaggering man's forehead.

David's slinger skill—that skill of seemingly little value—turns human history on its head. The now-victorious Israelites chase the Old Testament's quintessential bad guys to the gates of Goliath's hometown.

"Yeah, I remember the story."

Those winning smiles, however, don't last long. Later, David is hunted like an animal by the most powerful person in the land—the jealous, maniacal King Saul. And for the next decade or so, this obedient shepherd is on the run, hiding in caves and surviving off the land.

Then at the perfect time, this hero-turned-fugitive gets a new job. Any guess?

"Senior shepherd?"

Incredibly, anointed and now more than prepared for the role, David becomes the second king of Israel. Roll the credits:

GOD

As you look ahead in your own life, take an infusion of inspiration from this familiar story. Don't live another day with a confused view of who you are. Never again take your lunch pail, hard hat, or latest fashions to a worksite without supreme purpose. And in line with the broader message of these pages, get your boots or shoes or even slippers on solid ground regarding what work and the workplace can be.

"Got it."

Now, before we get too far along, let's get clear on what this thing called work is all about. In his book *Work, The Meaning of Your Life—A Christian Perspective*, Lester DeKoster wrote, "Work is the form in which we make ourselves useful to others."[1]

"That's it? That's the whole definition of work?"

No, there's more. As a sacred responsibility, your work should glorify God and uplift others. Jesus said the two most important commandments in Scripture are to love God with all your heart, soul, and mind and to love your neighbor as yourself (Matthew 22:37-39). In the marketplace, as an expression of your love, to love well is to work well. These commands establish the purpose of your work and should guide everything you do in your labor. Rightly considered, then, your work isn't just what you do in a job; it's what you intentionally do with your living. That's what work is.

"Are you talking about my job too?"

Yes, I'm talking about *all* work.

"But how is **my** *job a sacred responsibility? I don't work for a church, and I won't be shepherding anytime soon. Besides, for the most part, isn't work just something you do because someone gives you money to do it?"*

I understand what you're saying. I do. But here's what's troubling: If you put your job into a little economic-exchange box—that is, *I'll give you my time and effort if you give me something in return*—you won't realize the radical power of labor or grasp the breathtaking potential of work in God's plan.

"Uh, breathtaking potential?"

Yes! And during our time together, I aim to transform your thinking about work. That's because the God who "determines the number of the stars and calls them each by name" (Psalm 147:4) is the same God who sets the marketplace in motion, determines the number of occupations that exist, and calls by name the person He means to have each job. The Lord who created and sustains the universe and everything in it is the same Lord who creates, guides, and sustains the workplace and the many tasks in it. The Creator who spins objects in orbit and "stretches out the heavens" (Job 9:8) and "performs wonders that cannot be fathomed" (Job 9:10) is the same Creator who wants to use you in His marketplace.

Indeed, the everlasting Father has work for you to do specifically, and this unique work is a blessing. As Pastor Maltbie Babcock said more than a hundred years ago, "Be strong! We are not here to play, to dream, to drift; we have hard work to do, and loads to lift; shun not the struggle—face it; 'tis God's gift."[2]

"My work is a blessing...a gift?"

Yes, work is possibly the most bewildering, truly remarkable, and utterly time-consuming blessing you'll ever receive.

"Bewildered? That's how I feel when I get a fruitcake for Christmas."

I get it. If you feel bewildered about work, you're certainly not alone in feeling that way. Martin Luther, a leader in the Protestant Reformation centuries ago, once said, "The world does not consider labor a blessing." He added, "Therefore, it flees and hates it." But he also said, "The pious who fear the Lord, labor with a ready and cheerful heart; for they know God's commandment and will…Your work is a very sacred matter. God delights in it, and through it He wants to bestow His blessing on you."[3]

In the face of average, upsetting, or seemingly lousy work, I know my words can come off as out of touch and mockable. They're certainly easier to type than to cherish on a shop floor. But seeing all work as a blessing is possible when we recognize God's passion for what we do each day!

So if the work you do is bewildering, reflect on whether you believe the Holy One really says, *You're on your own.*

Attend to my words if you think what you're doing is a waste of time.

Press pause if you labor each day as if your job isn't worth your time or God's attention.

But then as we take a closer look at you and your work, get ready to learn more about God's love for you and the indisputable worthiness of *all* your labor.

Oh, and just in case you've ever wondered, it's not true that the world has only one fruitcake that people just keep passing around.

———— FURTHER REFLECTION AND APPLICATION ————

David's well-honed skill in slinging stones altered history, but his well-rehearsed songs made an impact on a nation forevermore. Among all pleasant-sounding options, King Saul sought David's musical abilities to soothe his demon-haunted mind (1 Samuel 16:14-23). With his music, David moved from the shepherds' hills and an audience of distant stars to the royal courts and an audience with his country's first king.

The everlasting Lord had a plan for David that involved years of herding sheep, slinging stones, and singing songs. So let me ask you—with no concern for the apparent value of the task, hobby, or activity—what are you doing today to lay the groundwork for tomorrow? No matter how silly or average your undertakings may seem, offer your time, practice, and experiences to our Lord in prayer. He has a plan for *you*.

WORK IS *WORK*

Wanted: Young, skinny, wiry fellows. Not over 18. Must be expert riders, willing to risk death daily. Orphans preferred.

These words come from an 1860 help wanted ad for the Pony Express in a California newspaper. I'm not sure many of today's children, who say some amazing things about their aspirations, would aspire to such a position.

In the photoblog *Humans of New York*, a young child says, "I want to be a mailman so I can let people know it's their birthday." A little girl declares, "I want to be a fairy when I grow up." When asked the best part of being a fairy, she answers, "Flying around with your friends." Another child shouts, "I want to be an astronaut!" When asked the hardest part about being an astronaut, he responds, "Pressing the right buttons at the right time!"

These comments are pure in the way only a child's can be. We smile at the rosy notions and romanticized innocence about labor, and we're reminded that dreams appear more achievable—and work seems more fun—from the outlook of a schoolyard.

For many young kids, their dream is to work—until they get their first job. No kid dreams of just trying to make a living, but (sorry to rain on the parade) for some of them, that dream job will never come true. When the children quoted in the blog join the marketplace, the little girl won't flutter around with her friends, and they'll all agree that work has its share of struggles.

Worse, when work is just a job or just a way to make a buck, tasks are a burden and work is just work.

If you have a job right now, tune into the conversations around you. Unlike if you listen to idealistic kids, you'll hear angst-riddled hurt. Too many workers muddle along—just working to live—and, candidly, many of them are none too happy about it.

In response, cheap shots abound.

Musicians take steady jabs at the workplace. The ironically named Johnny Paycheck, in his recording of "Take This Job and Shove It," sang about how he was walking off his job in a factory, where, in his opinion, his foreman and line boss weren't exactly deserving of respect. Even cartoonists prop up the fun house mirror and sneak in punches. Scott Adams is best known as the creator of the character Dilbert. His books sell for a reason—they throw in the towel for the work experience.

At work, you might hear sentiments like, "I'm just killing time until I find something else." I saw a T-shirt proclaiming, *Step aside, coffee; this is a job for alcohol!* in this same TGIF vein. Comedian Drew Carey once joked, "Oh, you hate your job? Why didn't you say so? There's a support group for that. It's called everybody, and they meet at the bar." Extending the sarcasm, here's another slogan I've seen: *If I just had one hour to live, I'd spend it in this joyless cubicle, because then it would feel like an eternity.*

And who can forget the travails of a faithful man named—seriously, of all things, *J-O-B*—Job?

If you combine these dour takes, it seems only poetic that you can't spell *laboring* without *boring* and that *work* is a four-letter word. Basically, if many people had their way, they would heap work unceremoniously onto a dumpster fire and leave it there to burn.

"Yeah, most days, I'd say the best part of work is the ride home afterward. Can I count that? Why is work such a drag at times?"

Well, just past the middle of Genesis 3, after the turnout of a talking serpent and the subsequent "fall," the same Hebrew word for "labor" is used for both the toil of work and the pain in childbirth. Going forward from this infamous, thanks-for-nothing moment, these basic parts of life—working and bearing children—would be infused with strain and pain.

Yes, these last several paragraphs are a bit doom and gloom. But understand that work itself is not a result of Adam's so-called thorny "curse" in which he was to eat his bread by the sweat of his brow. In his book *Why Business Matters to God*, business school dean Jeff Van Duzer said it this way:

> Christians often incorrectly perceive work as having been assigned to
> human beings as punishment for Adam and Eve's disobedience in the
> Garden of Eden. Nothing could be further from the truth. The call and
> the opportunity to work were imbedded into the very fabric of human
> beings as they were first designed by God. Adam and Eve were assigned
> work in the Garden from the beginning.[1]

No, your labor is not a regrettable consequence of this dustup, blame game, and major rift that followed. Countless laborers talk about work as if it were Hades with pay, but as part of the abundant life (John 10:10), work is good—something good that God has given us to do. Though these words may come off as woefully clueless or a terrible mistake in judgment, I repeat, work is good!

That stated, work suffers from much more than horrible public relations. The ensuing struggles and groan-and-swipe-left sentiments are a result of this "curse." Not being naive or witless—and stating what's been known since wearable fig leaves were the rage—work today is not as originally mandated.

"But work is hard to avoid."

That didn't stop some people from trying. At the time of the New Testament, the Romans and Greeks considered the material world hazardous to eternal well-being, and they viewed labor, particularly manual effort, as an unmitigated barrier to their quest for truth. To them, work had no redeeming features, and unless you were a slave, any labor that required bending, lifting, or using your hands was to be avoided.

Basically, having a physical job was admitting to your friends that you'd given up. "Hey, come on, put down that stinking shovel and have some self-respect!" comes to mind. And it's safe to say that philosopher Aristotle and his friends never stooped to lay blacktop or sweated as roofers in July.

You see, Aristotle believed that to be unemployed was great fortune (um, please don't rely on this at home) because it permitted a person to participate in a life of contemplation apart from the care of work. With applause and approval from deep thinkers all over, he reasoned that a purely contemplative life was the happiest life.[2]

But take a moment to reflect on how this sentiment differs from what theologians refer to as the cultural mandate (Genesis 1:28), the expectation for us to be fruitful and multiply and "subdue" the earth (i.e., harness the natural world). The cultural mandate, which God gave to Adam and Eve, also directs you to be His representative right now! Understanding this ongoing mandate is core to the biblical doctrine of work.[3]

So, influenced by Aristotle, the reigning intellectuals of their day stroked their chins and posed stately questions like, "Work—hmm, why?" As far as they were concerned, contemplation or worthwhile activity—certainly not physical labor—was the whole point of life.

Now, in stark contrast (and in line with Hebrew teachings), *Yeshua ben Yosef*, or Jesus son of Joseph, came to show that all work is worthy and that the material world is God's creation. Living in an area overly influenced by this Greek thinking (and not fitting the prevailing narrative), Jesus chose to work side by side with His earthly father as a precision-focused carpenter. For love's sake, Jesus became "flesh" (John 1:14) and sought a physically demanding blue-collar job that no self-respecting Greek of that time would take.

The incarnate deity, Jesus, was a craftsman.

Joy to the world! The Lord is come: Let earth receive her king! And with His messianic mission and astonishing power, our King of kings shall…uh, get paid to craft and measure things? And as a model of patience and contentment, the prophesied Messiah who strode where angels trod…shall work on His knees with sweat on His brow?

Yes, this One who walked on water embraced the halo-free human experience as a down-and-dirty wage earner. "To us a child is born, to us a son is given, and the government will be on his shoulders. And he will be called Wonderful Counselor, Mighty God, Everlasting Father, Prince of Peace" (Isaiah 9:6)—and a common work tool will be in His calloused hands.

"Hmm. So how long was Jesus a craftsman?"

Being a carpenter wasn't part of a cameo appearance or an occasional hobby. His employment wasn't just tried on for size. From the age of 12, as part of His family's small-town building business, Jesus worked with devices to fashion rock or wood into useful objects. Before His public ministry, the Great "I AM" humbled Himself in obedience to God the Father and spent 18 years bidding jobs, constructing, and redeeming local structures in need of repair and handiwork.

It might sound crude to say, but Jesus knew the ins and outs of business, responded to the ill whims of customers, and exchanged trade services and products for cash. Sure, if your sole focus has centered on Jesus as a sage, deity, messiah, political rebel, or prophetic revolutionary, it may take some effort to wrap your mind around this reality of Jesus Christ as a first-century workhand. But in *God at Work: Live Each Day with Purpose*, banking executive Ken Costa noted the following:

> We can easily imagine Jesus purchasing wood and nails, making a window or door, negotiating a price, and selling his work. In these hidden years, Jesus must have come into contact with a cross-section of the community in Nazareth. This is reflected in his teaching, which includes references to workers in the vineyard, meetings with tax collectors, dealings with agents, and discussions about money, livestock, and property. He did not come to give us a new form of spiritual life disconnected from the world. He came to continue and restore the patterns of work and service initiated by his Father.[4]

In my Google search of jobs today, only a few job titles came up in each of these three listings: the worst jobs, the lowest-paid jobs, and the most-dangerous jobs. Startlingly—and it gave me chills—of all the jobs listed, carpenter was among the few that hit today's "bad job trifecta"—it was on each list.

All things considered, then, not that much has changed for carpenters in 2,000 years! In 1966, Tim Hardin released a song about a man wondering if his job was a significant barrier to being loved. In the many years to follow, it was covered by numerous artists. What wage-earning kingdom assignment could be so bad? The title of the song is "If I Were a Carpenter."

Do you know the most respected job of Jesus's day? Was it a king or maybe a priest?

"Yeah, why didn't Jesus work in one of those roles?"

That's a good question. He certainly didn't work as an earthly king or priest. Have you noticed that the job Jesus had before His public ministry led to sneers—just like David's job as a shepherd had? At the synagogue, the religious leaders scoffed, "'He's just a carpenter, the son of Mary and the brother of James, Joseph, Judas, and Simon. And his sisters live right here among us.' They were deeply offended and refused to believe in him" (Mark 6:3 NLT).

To these professionally outraged men, this provincial artisan lacked credibility on almost every important matter. Here's a paraphrase of this same text: "In the next breath they were cutting him down: 'He's just a carpenter—Mary's boy. We've known him since he was a kid. We know his brothers, James, Justus, Jude, and Simon, and his sisters. Who does he think he is?'" (MSG).

With their pious smirks, these men muttered Jesus's job title to dismiss Him. And with what we see here, is it any surprise that, at His crucifixion years later, Jesus was derided with what was intended as a dismissive job title? As you may recall, those who killed Him whittled *King of the Jews* on a board and slammed it on the wooden cross above His head.

"That's brutal. So Jesus knew all about work."

He did. Jesus's daily work experience on earth was basically like yours and mine. Except for the Sabbath, the sun rose and the sun set on yet another workday—and the hammering work was tough. His grueling employment is another part of His being human. And Jesus the Christ—His name and title—can relate to your work trials because He faced them too.

The Hebrew word *Immanuel* means "God with us." And when I hear it, I'm reminded of God with us "in manual" labor. The author of Hebrews 4:15 says Jesus was "tempted in every way, just as we are." I like this paraphrase: "We don't have a priest who is out of touch with our reality. He's been through weakness and testing, experienced it all—all but the sin" (MSG).

"He's walked a mile in our scuffed work boots."

Yes, and this helps to explain why many of Jesus's parables—targeting such things as laborers, construction (Matthew 7:24-27), family-owned businesses (Matthew 21:28-31), and uses of money (Luke 15:11-16)—were set in the workplace. Consider that in the New Testament, of Jesus's 132 public appearances, 122 were in the marketplace. And of the 52 parables this perfect, first-century workhand told, 45 had a workplace context.

Further, of 40 miracles in the book of Acts, 39 were in the marketplace, and more than half of Jesus's reported teaching ministry arose out of issues posed by others in the context of daily life experience.[5] It should be no surprise, then, that each of the men He called as disciples was comfortable in the marketplace. None were leaders in a temple or synagogue.

"What did they do?"

It's interesting that we know the specific jobs held by only some of the disciples. Three seasoned freshwater-lake fishermen (Peter, James, and John) were the closest to Jesus, but four fishermen in total were seeking net income. Peter and his brother Andrew, business partners with their father, were both casting fishing nets into a lake when Jesus called them. James and John were busy with the routine task of mending nets when recruited to join the group. And Matthew (also called Levi) was befriended by Jesus with two words—"Follow me"—while balancing the books in a nearby tax collector's booth (Matthew 9:9).

Jesus's genealogy in the book of Matthew includes laborers of many types, though. And to help you relate even more to His Word, God provides examples of trades, means of employment, and more than 100 unique jobs.

Yet time has forgotten if the incumbent breadwinners were on a fast track, considered high potential, or just biding their time. And any framed degrees, sketched certifications, or portraits hung in halls turned to dust centuries ago. Also, if one of these doers felt underemployed for whatever reason, it would be news to you and me.

"What do you mean by underemployed?"

These days, "underemployed" describes people who are underutilized considering the experience and talents they bring to the table. Have you had a job that challenged your sense of dignity? Or do you have a job like that now? If so, you know what I'm talking about. And when (not if) your self-respect takes a blow or you're marginalized in the workplace, remember that the Son of God was often excluded and humiliated as well.

Let me pose a question you've probably never heard: Can you imagine our Immanuel, humbled in obedience, working today in an ordinary greasy-spoon restaurant and asking, "Would you like fries with that?"

It's a strange question, and it may have elicited a weird image in your mind. But ponder this: Even if He worked as a country's president or prime minister, the Son of the living God, this King of kings and Lord of lords, would be ridiculously underemployed. In many ways, it's more than amazing to consider that God worked in human form in this world at all!

And remember this: The fact that Jesus Christ labored for several years in a rough-and-tumble role in an imperfect marketplace is core to His relatable story and central to God's redemptive plan. The sinless Son of Man worked right in our midst, but no one awaiting the Deliverer (or a military messiah or commander who would challenge Rome and conquer Israel's enemies) expected it to go down quite like this.

"So what can I expect in my days ahead?"

Well, here's a news flash you won't see on any business website or channel: Your worksite is the center of a spiritual battle. The evil perpetrator who wreaked havoc near the beginning of time is joined by other dark forces today. This means your character, judgment, and faith were improperly fitted with bull's-eyes and will be targeted at every turn.

Deceiving everyone on earth, the most cunning of all creatures lies and jests from the depth of his being. With only a bare outline of work experience, the devil will muse, *This job is no good. You deserve so much more.* And at just the wrong time, the "ruler of the kingdom of the air" (Ephesians 2:2) will whisper, *Be sure to leave your faith at the door.* On the prowl and desperate to cause wreckage, the original identity thief will also spew, *Go ahead. No one will notice!* And where resistance rages, he'll say, *Come on. You? Look at your past. You can't possibly make a difference.*

Anticipate getting hit with shots like these from the one who seeks to destroy and from the stygian depths of hell for as long as you work. And if what you're doing is just a job to you, your work experience may provide little more than tedium sprinkled with sporadic moments of fear.

But at the same time, here's what's exciting: As a believer, your work isn't just work. What you're doing isn't just a job. Throughout your entire work life, you'll experience amazing highs during personal glimpses of work as it was intended to be.

"But you said the world of work was ruined."

Let's circle back to the beginning of Scripture. Before the middle of Genesis 3 and mankind's introduction to strain and pain, we catch a fleeting glimpse of work as it was designed to be. For this short-lived stretch, work was central to a newly created paradise. Creation and work were filled with beauty, order, and perfect peace.

Not holding anything back, in the headliner opening *In the beginning*, God is instantly engaged in elevating work. Not burying the lead, He's shown as the primary worker. He plants a garden, places Adam and Eve there as image bearers, and—after establishing the Sabbath and resting—enters the garden Himself to dwell and to actively provide each day.

Can you visualize what it would have been like to be there? Can you see yourself next to the Creator while He works in and through you?

Now, can you recall the ten words from the start of this book?

"God can use anyone, and He wants to use you."

Right! The world of work was damaged when sin came into the world, but God loves the world of work, and He wants you and me to contribute to it. Time and again, you'll be called to help the marketplace inch closer to the way the world was meant to be. So as His hands and feet, be sure to embrace the workplace and improve what you see. If something can be done better, do it better. You've been thoughtfully placed where you are to help establish order from chaos and to enhance how work gets done.

Central to loving God is loving the people He puts in your life—even at work. Sometimes you'll serve the Lord by helping others with their tasks. Other times, as you follow His lead, the workplace will be your best opportunity to share the "good news." Over time, your faith shown in action (see Matthew 5:16) may influence others unlike any church podcast or multisite sermon.

It makes no difference if you're a homemaker, home builder, farmer, or pharmacy tech. From landscapes to skyscrapers, no matter where you labor, our Lord Almighty doesn't need a steeple to accomplish His purposes.

"But what if I just really hate what I'm doing?"

Answering that question takes some lengthy discussion. See the "What If I Hate What I'm Doing?" section on page 143.

——————— FURTHER REFLECTION AND APPLICATION ———————

Consider the following set of questions: Of all possible trades, why was our Immanuel a carpenter? Don't you think it's beyond stunning that the Savior of the world was—at different times—a newborn in a cattle stall, a blue-collar worker, and a crucified Messiah?

At the time of the Gospels, shepherds—the lowest in occupation and social class—were so distrusted and despised that their testimony wasn't accepted in court. So isn't it that much more amazing that angelic hosts appeared to a delegation of shepherds to pronounce Jesus's birth? That as planned, universe-shaking tidings of comfort and joy were shared with provincial herders lacking credibility on nearly every important matter—like David was?

Please read John 10:1-11, about the Good Shepherd and His sheep, and ponder how our Lord works in your workplace.

3

WHAT'S THE POINT?

I n his book *The Wright Brothers*, David McCullough tells us the journalists and reporters at Orville and Wilbur's hometown newspapers almost completely neglected the story of the duo's historic achievement—the maiden flight of the *Wright Flyer*. That might have you wondering about how we can all sometimes fail to see big news. Even when it's right in front of us, sometimes we're caught off guard, fail to pick up what's really going on, or completely miss the point.

The Wrights, who made their first successful engine-powered flight in Kitty Hawk, North Carolina, offered the story to their hometown papers back in Dayton, Ohio, where they operated a bicycle shop and had designed the plane. But the city editor at the *Dayton Daily Journal* showed no interest. As a result, no mention was made of this incredible story in his newspaper the following day—though it did receive brief attention in the *Dayton Daily News* on an inside page somewhere.

Writing later, James Cox, publisher of the *Dayton Daily News*, recalled the reports and telegrams coming "to our office that the airship had been in the air over the Huffman Prairie…but our news staff would not believe the stories. Nor did they ever take the pains to go out and see." And when Dan Kumler, the city editor of the *Dayton Daily News*, was asked why it took so long to report the amazing accomplishments taking place nearby, he surmised, "I guess the truth is that we were just plain dumb."[1]

Like these reporters, do we sometimes "miss it" at work? That is, do we fail to see the point of it all? And what if we approach work as mere tasks and never go beyond that?

"You're saying there must be a better way."

I am.

How would you finish this sentence? *I work to* _____.

The subject is there, and so is the verb. Now select your top three reasons for working from the following choices:

Make money	Stay involved	Help with the family business
Get health benefits	Make a name for myself	Compete and win
Please my mom	Get someone off my back	Love others
Challenge the status quo	Become famous	Pay off student loans
Stay busy	Please my dad	Make the world a better place
Buy stuff	Learn new things	Fend off boredom
Provide for my family	Hide the pain	Stay out of trouble
Have something to share	Follow my passion	Get out of the house
Act justly	Glorify God	Use my talents
Advance justice	Do what interests me	Get ahead
Care for the less fortunate	Help others	Be a part of something
Survive	Save the environment	Make a difference
Pay the bills	Gain status	Help those who come after me
Be with other people	Keep up with others	Be happy
Feel more secure	Gain power	Make others happy
Pass the time	Contribute to my field	Um, I don't know
Be loyal to my employer	Prove something	

We'll come back to your top three reasons at the end of this chapter. But next, here's a work-related question that's the most important one my gray matter can generate. Adding to its significance, your answer affects everything else about your work.

Are you ready?

"Sure."

Here's the question: Who do you work for?

If you're like many people, what popped into your brain was *My supervisor* or *The person I report to.*

In the course of a day, you can be bossed around by a lot of people. From landlords and grumpy siblings to flight attendants and local politicians, it seems many individuals believe it's their responsibility to tell you what to do. At work, though, you may take orders from one or more watchful supervisors, and when they say "Jump!" you may squirm and respond, "How high?"

Ultimately, Scripture is clear on this question—and the answer isn't your boss, your boss's boss, or the department VP. In the end, you don't work for anyone who has accrued more tenure, makes more money, relies on you for stuff, or stands a rung higher on the company ladder.

And you won't see the answer staring back at you in the mirror. You won't gain insights from a self-help book. Even if you're freelancing, side-hustling, self-employed, or an entrepreneur, your work life isn't about you. ("Me" is a good guess, though, as the interest in looking out for "number one" certainly predates selfies.) And like a magician with a handkerchief in one hand and a coin palmed in the other, the deceiver has tricked many into focusing on the wrong object: themselves.

But the answer to this question is both simple and radical.

"Okay, who is it?"

God.

"Okay, but..."

He alone is the source and ultimate goal of your work!

You won't find this truth in your employee handbook. And no, it's not tucked away in a company policy statement. Not mincing words, with no shade of subtlety, and often repeating the message for emphasis, God says the following in His Word:

- "We must serve wholeheartedly, as if we're serving the Lord instead of people" (Ephesians 6:7).
- "God created us for his glory" (Isaiah 43:7).
- "Whatever we do should be to God's glory" (1 Corinthians 10:31).
- "Each person is given something to do that shows who God is" (1 Corinthians 12:7).

Together, these succinct verses tell us who we work for. It doesn't matter if you're full- or part-time. It's unimportant whether you're scrubbing floors or wearing scrubs. From a call center to the center stage, work is more than mere economic exchange. And from a makeshift lemonade stand to a cleanup in aisle two, everything you do is ultimately done to serve God. (For more about whether God cares about what happens even in workplaces like a supermarket or retail outlet store, see *A* under "Chapter 3: What's the Point?" in Going Deeper.)

That everything we do is ultimately done to serve God is the often-missed point—and it changes everything! He created you for a relationship with Him and to work for His honor alone.

The Bible contains several general calls to faith with a particular calling to work. (We'll talk about vocational calling in chapter 4.) In 1 Peter 4:10, we're told, "Each of you should use whatever gift you have received to serve others, as faithful stewards of God's grace in its various forms." That means if you're physically able, you're expected to serve your neighbors—even your neighbor at work.

Far beyond bad etiquette—or a bad day—turning your back on God's call is wrong. Come to think of it, you don't need anyone to tell you it's never wise to reject anything that's both a blessing and a call.

"Most of this is far different from what I hear every day."

Don't expect the world's messages to align with the divine—they rarely do.

Here's the difference: As a believer, you seek to work *with* God above all else and view this time as eternally significant. In contrast, the world seeks to work for everything *but* God and views much of time at a job a waste.

If you ever struggle with ultimate purpose (as I do), consider Jesus's main motivation. His definitive purpose as a carpenter was the same as yours: He worked to glorify God. This truth gives ultimate purpose to all work!

No part of the daily grind is too obscure for your diligence and His care. If you're involved, God's Spirit is involved too. God is there in the starry night, flaming flowers, and snow-covered mountains, and He's involved just as much as you perform repetitive, run-of-the-mill tasks. As a believer with a radically different outlook, with hope in sight, you give your all because the dullness of sheer duty can reflect the palette-worthy beauty of service.

So let me ask you this: Have you ever had a really nasty chore to do or a terribly monotonous job?

"Of course."

Okay. Given my extended time in the restaurant business, let's consider the supposed unskilled and ordinary task of making a fast-food hamburger.

It's not news that "no frills" food-prep work such as burger flipping isn't many people's aspiration. Having vigorously recruited and selected for this type of high-turnover position around the globe over many years, I know firsthand that these jobs can be surprisingly tough. Typically, these workers aren't paid well, and their jobs often lack the "it" factor with friends.

If you're a team member today, a quality-focused restaurant manager—hoping to change how you view and do your work—might say to you, "Would you serve that hamburger to your mom?" But what if we raised the bar, kicked it up a notch, and asked, "How would you make a hamburger if you saw yourself as serving the Lord?"

As a believer, with some elbow grease and a focus on excellence, you would ensure the food was more than deserving of the name Hamburger Deluxe. Shades of mediocrity? No, for you, *just okay* just isn't okay. It's a basic question of "Lordship." Certainly, for the One "robed in majesty" (Psalm 93:1), pleasing work can happen while wearing a grimy uniform. And the restaurant manager and paying customers would absolutely love your through-the-roof product quality.

During each shift of every workday still to come, the One known as "the bread of life" (John 6:35) will work in and through employees in this type of job to serve food or "daily bread" to each hungry patron. So tell me, if making a fast-food burger is worthwhile, what on earth isn't?

"I guess all work is worth doing."

Yes, it absolutely is, and you don't need to guess. All labor—whether dismissed or respected, voluntary or for pay—is worthwhile! Even the grubbiest task and anonymous toil aren't done in vain. (For more insight about this concept, see *B* under "Chapter 3: What's the Point?" in Going Deeper.)

Consider a service-sector employee tiptoeing on a slippery floor, wearing a stained uniform, and flipping beef patties while surrounded by a surplus of sauces and cheese slices as you hear the perspective of Paul the faithful tentmaker. From prison, he wrote, "Work willingly at whatever you do, as though you were working for the Lord rather than for people" (Colossians 3:23 NLT).

In other words, everything we do matters, and if your work didn't matter to God, He wouldn't have called you to do it. Absolutely nothing He gives us is without value, and every job displays a unique and beautiful aspect of His character.

Right now, make a note of your most trying responsibilities and reflect on this prayer:

> *Thank You, God, for giving me these simple tasks.*
> *Help me to see these responsibilities as blessings—*
> *Because many times I don't.*
> *May I never forget the sacred nature of my work.*
> *Teach me to be grateful in all circumstances—*
> *As I am Your work in progress.*

With certainty, God is just as much the God of the ordinary as He is the Lord of the unmatched and extraordinary. In the *Institutes of the Christian Religion*, hundreds of years ago, Protestant reformer John Calvin surmised, "No task will be [seen as] so sordid and base, provided you obey your calling in it, that it will not shine and be reckoned very precious in God's sight."[2] And this is heartening because most of us don't do novel or exciting things at work. In the last century, pastor and author A.W. Tozer shared, "Let us practice the fine art of making every work a priestly ministration. Let us believe that God is in all our simple deeds and learn to find Him there."[3]

Martin Luther King Jr., minister and US civil rights activist, stated, "If a man is called to be a street-sweeper, he should sweep streets even as Michelangelo painted, or Beethoven played music, or Shakespeare wrote poetry. He should sweep streets so well that all the hosts of heaven and earth will pause to say, here lived a great street-sweeper who did his job well."[4]

To remind you of your high standard every time you punch in or swipe your security badge, use the following acronym to summarize what authentic work is about. Whether folding laundry, assisting a customer, or scrubbing spaghetti sauce off a sofa, let all else fade in comparison as you

Worship
Our
Risen
King.

"I never considered some tasks that worthwhile."

I'm glad to have challenged your thinking!

The ultimate purpose of our work applies to any task. (See *C* under "Chapter 3: What's the Point?" in Going Deeper for our lengthy side conversation about whether all jobs are equal.)

Nothing has changed about work except how you relate to it. Whatever you do, put an end to the notion of a senseless task or dead-end job—and do your best to respond to your lofty work standard: *Everything I do is for God's glory.* (See *D* under "Chapter 3: What's the Point?" in Going Deeper to learn more about why this isn't just a platitude or outdated notion.)

All jobs bright and beautiful, all labor great and small, and all things wise and wonderful—the Lord God made them all, right? So, then, if you love restaurant work, keep doing it with distinction. It's amazing to see a laborer in a so-called ordinary job doing numbingly routine things day after day with a cheerful and pleasing heart.

"Agree! So, does the purpose of our work ever change?"

No, our higher-order purpose never changes. As you progress in your work life, though you may find more meaning in certain work, your ultimate purpose is constant. Your purpose isn't in your work or in anything that comes from it!

You don't move from success to significance by changing what you do. You won't find ultimate purpose when switching from a for-profit to a nonprofit organization. And please don't wait until later in life—a second half—to seek definitive purpose in your pursuits. Because in any form of labor—from investment banking to a caring profession—the whole point of work is to point wholly to Him. In other words, your work life is without highest purpose until it finds purpose in God.

(And for the loan shark, drug dealer, and rip-off artist—as well as any others reading these words who are involved in some immoral, uninspired stuff—put down what you're doing, listen for God's leading, and get another job. God has a better work life for you. He loves you as you are, but He loves you too much to let you stay that way.)

"Though money talks, only God calls."

You got that right!

Now, let's shift gears and move ahead. Read the statements below:

- If you go outside with wet hair, you'll catch cold.
- If you keep making that face, one day it'll be stuck like that—forever.
- If you swallow your gum, it will stay in your stomach for seven years.

Do you recognize any of these? You know, sometimes even ruses or silly lies can affect your behavior. I still don't swallow my gum, just to be sure.

Lies, as with their living distributors, come in all sizes and types. What all lies share is a casual or broken relationship with the truth. Sadly, most deception targets what's meaningful and somehow distorts it as meaningless. Some misinformation is pretty harmless; borrow a word from your grandparents and call it "malarkey" if you will. Other lies, though, are more serious—from slander at work to perjury in the courtroom.

The deceiver is the source of all these lies. His preoccupation nowadays isn't with malarkey or urban legends, and maybe not even with slander or perjury. No, as part of the spiritual battle, the evil perpetrator has more important stuff to go after.

His obsession is your mind.

"Seriously, what's up with that?"

The deceiver wants to control everything about you. And the best way to influence your habits is to influence your thinking. If he can alter the soft stuff between your ears, the father of all lies knows his desired behaviors will follow.

Now, well beyond the fibs and white lies—and past even the more serious deception—at the extreme end of this dark spectrum we find a solitary lie causing untold damage. This stronghold is nestled in with posturing, twisted agendas and rabid pursuits of power.

Take a moment to stare right at it and understand what's to be won or lost. Truth be told, this falsehood muddies the minds of billions of working people every day.

"What's the lie?"

God's not here.

But you don't have to believe this lie.

To get your mind right, let's be completely clear on this:

Everything belongs to God.

Our world belongs to God.

Your work belongs to God, and God is in your work.

Highlight the last three sentences with the brightest fluorescent color you have and do your best to remember them. At risk of being repetitive, but to ensure there's no doubt, let's read the following verses in Scripture:

- "The earth is the Lord's, and everything in it" (1 Corinthians 10:26).
- "The earth is the LORD's, and all it contains, the world, and those who dwell in it" (Psalm 24:1 NASB).
- "If I go up to the heavens, you are there; if I make my bed in the depths, you are there" (Psalm 139:8).
- "To the LORD your God belong the heavens, even the highest heavens, the earth and everything in it" (Deuteronomy 10:14).

"What if someone has never gone to work expecting to meet God there? Um, I'm asking for a friend."

Well, He's there anyway! Abraham Kuyper, a Dutch theologian, said, "There is not a square inch in the whole domain of our human existence over which Christ, who is Sovereign over *all*, does not cry: 'Mine!'"[5] This includes every single location your pumps, sandals, high-tops, steel-toed shoes, or work boots can go. That's because every inch of every mill and mall, salon and saloon, classroom and courtroom was claimed as sacred space long ago. Each cubicle, factory floor, watercooler, laundry pile, toy-strewn basement, and carefully built flying machine and floating vessel—every work sphere and sector along with every bit and byte—belong to Him every second, minute, hour, and day of the year.

Reflecting on these certainties, if Jacob, who had the vision of a heavenly stairway resting on a middle-of-nowhere rocky spot, slogged side by side with you today, he might shout, "Surely the LORD is in this place...How awesome is this place!" (Genesis 28:16-17).

Author Annie Dillard once asked, "What is the difference between a cathedral and a physics lab? Are not they both saying: Hello?"[6] To be certain, yes, God is in both the cathedral and the physics lab. He's revealed in Saturn's rings (see *E* under "Chapter 3: What's the Point?" in Going Deeper for some lyric inspiration), the lilies of the field, and every hospital delivery room. And let's see here...well, the Lord also gloriously dwells in every gin joint, dingy hallway, lightless crack and crevice—and toxic workplace. Looking at Scripture, I'd say to Annie Dillard—and I think she'd agree—that in a sense *every* domain is saying: Hello.

That's because the truth is there's no place where God is not.

For those who like an analogy to underpin a point, I'll give you one: Work without God is like tango without two. (Remember, it takes two to tango.)

"Let me think about that."

Sure, go ahead and think about it. Then, along with all creation, use your outside voice to tell the world that God is preeminent and supreme over all—the material and the spiritual.

Look at it this way. Although He knocks on your door, the Lord doesn't need your invitation. No, the intimate invitation from Him is to leave your life and join Him as a participant in His work, not the other way around. Even when filled with bullying or seediness, your place of work is a place of divine encounter. Our Immanuel has been active there the entire time.

Earlier, I encouraged you to get ready to learn. And I promised to prod, challenge, and encourage you along the way, right? With that in mind and to reinforce a key point, I'll ask you a geography question: Before Mount Everest was discovered, what, based on altitude, was the tallest mountain on earth above sea level?

"I'm not sure. Just tell me."

The answer is Mount Everest. This mountain has been and will continue to be the tallest mountain on earth above sea level, apart from any discovery, acceptance, or belief. And yes, God has been and will continue to be in every single location, including where you work. This amazing truth doesn't depend on someone's discovery or belief. Nor can this truth be altered by lies. God has always been there, and He always will be, apart from anyone's thoughts on the matter.

Now think about God, your workplace, and you. Assume that each of these three is represented by a circle. With what we've covered here, how would you draw them to represent your day-in, day-out work experience? Would the circles overlap? Would they be different sizes? Would any circle stand alone?

In the following space, draw how you think these three circles interact. Go ahead. Give it a shot.

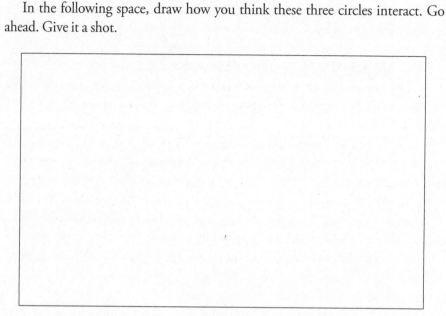

DIAGRAM 1

We'll call this the Puzzle of Work.

Obviously, God the Father doesn't murmur, *Nothing personal; it's just business.* And He'd never conclude, *It doesn't mean that much to Me to mean that much to you.* The Lord will never utter goodbye in the morning as you head out to wherever you go for what you do. He won't occasionally check in during the afternoon to see how you're doing. And He won't wait around to greet you when you return home. (That's your dog or cat's job.)

No, the Creator of this universe, who loves you dearly, doesn't wonder all day what you're doing, what you're thinking about, and what life's like for you. That's because, spilling over with goodness, He's with you the whole day through, just as He promises.

So wherever and whenever, know that God works in and through you. And thus, as believers, we find complete overlap between God and us. In the workplace, God's previous and current work meets your present response in full. The only other matter—and it's relatively less important—is the amount of overlap for you and your workplace.

"I hope it's not complete overlap! I have to be there enough as it is."

No, it's not a complete overlap. When you get to the last page of this chapter, look for the square there. An arrow points to the inspired intersection where you'll find God with you and your work. But as you consider the answer now, recall that, by grace, everything about you—including the heart at the center of your being—has been carefully stitched together by God's hands to join Him in specific tasks He arranged long ago.

Once again, this is affirmed in Ephesians 2:10: "We are God's handiwork"—think about that word, *handiwork*—"created in Christ Jesus to do good works, which God prepared in advance for us to do."

As your co-laborer, God is at work in you and through you to do the work He intends.

"Okay. I've thought about it, and I'll be sure to look at that square."

Great. Now, earlier, you chose your top three reasons for working from a list of choices. But before we discuss your choices, let me share a TV news account from Minneapolis-Saint Paul.

A retired man named Joe, who won nearly $12 million in the lottery, kept his snowplow job in his snowy state. He even serviced most of the ten accounts (accounts he committed to before he became a millionaire) for free to help people who needed it and using a Chevy pickup he'd bought used.[7] Joe and his wife made some big purchases with the money—another house and a motor home, for instance—but he seemed to have his priorities straight.

You may be in debt, nearly penniless, or otherwise, but God (*Jehovah-Jireh*, Genesis 22:14) knows all about your student-loan payments, your challenge balancing your checkbook, or the difficulty in keeping your daily priorities in check. And although a few become millionaires, He recognizes (as you must) that life doesn't get easier for most people as they get older because (just like their ears) their bills only get bigger.

Here's a simple action: Don't wait until you've paid your bills to get your priorities in order. Because guess what? You'll always be paying them.

Now tell me your top three reasons for working.

"To make money, get health benefits, and make a difference."

Your reasons as well as many of the choices from the *I work to* _____ list are fine. And in some form or fashion, your family and friends will likely applaud as you chase after those three goals. But like a sailor considers a smaller jib sail only after setting the main sail, view these reasons as background or secondary aims. That's because there's only one right answer for your first choice. No matter the circumstance, your first, unmatched reason for work must be to glorify God. Put God first, and value everything at work in relation to Him. He made you for His glory! As Paul tells us, "From him and through him and for him are all things. To him be the glory forever!" (Romans 11:36).

So if you're working first to chase after a check, ask God to help you with your priorities.

If you're primarily working for health benefits, reprioritize.

If you're putting in hours foremost to make a difference, reprioritize again.

Your life mirrors your priorities for living, and your job or career reflects your reasons for work. Tough times or not, helping you get your priorities in proper order is at the heart of what work is all about.

THE STUDENT

I work closely with Paul Sheeran. His daughter, Payton, a student at a Midwestern college, recently wrote this email to her friends at school. (Payton, thanks for letting me include it here.)

> Today I was reminded of the truth and importance of Colossians 3:23, "Work willingly at whatever you do, as though you were working for the Lord rather than for people," and wanted to share it with you guys: I'm taking an online class and there is a lot of work that we have to do outside of class.

It's not hard, just tedious and takes a long time. So far, I've worked for three hours on a little over half of the work that is due next week. As always, I've been putting forth my best effort.

Today though, I was talking to someone who took the class last semester, and he pretty much said the teacher doesn't even read over the work, but will give you an "A" as long as you have "words on a page." Upon first hearing this I was really frustrated. After all, I had put in a lot of time and effort to do the work and was now learning that I could have put in about a quarter of the effort and time and still gotten the same grade!

Not only did I feel like this was unfair, but I also felt like I had wasted my time. But the more I thought about it, God challenged me to think about who I was doing the work for. If I'm doing the work just to get a good grade or get praise from a teacher, then yeah, I probably wasted my time. But if I'm working for the Lord and only the Lord, then does He deserve anything less than my best?

If I'm truly "working for the Lord rather than for people" then it shouldn't matter how hard/easy the teacher grades, how much the assignment is worth, or applied in a different context—how much money I will make or who will see my "good work." If I'm truly working for the Lord I should give my best at everything I do, because He deserves nothing less!

So, then, who are *you* working for?

FURTHER REFLECTION AND APPLICATION

When you pray for "daily bread," you are praying for everything that contributes to your having and enjoying your daily bread. You must open up and expand your thinking so that it reaches not only as far as the flour bin and baking oven, but also out over the broad fields, the farmlands, and the entire country that produces, processes, and conveys to us our daily bread.

That's Martin Luther writing in what's called his Large Catechism.

To see this in action, visit a local coffee shop or quick-service restaurant. Pay attention to the many seemingly unimportant yet beautifully stitched-together tasks. Recognize each of the workers by name and the interconnected tasks that are part of planning, sourcing, producing, distributing, inventorying, preparing, and serving your food or drink, and then ponder God's caring ways.

Also read 1 Thessalonians 5:18: "Give thanks in all circumstances; for this is God's will for you in Christ Jesus." Notice how Scripture encourages you in this. God is calling us to be thankful *in* our work circumstances, not necessarily *for* them. And there's a big difference! Ask God to help you be thankful in your work circumstances no matter what they may be.

Here's the answer to the Puzzle of Work:

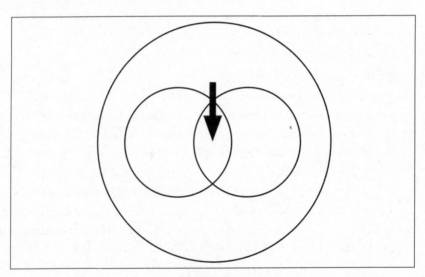

DIAGRAM 2

4

YOUR WHY

Let me tell you something. You are completely amazing! You are awesome, and yes, I mean it. It's crazy, but you are!

awkward silence

I know.

From an early age, you've been told you're special—repeatedly. (When our older son was three, my wife put him in time-out for misbehaving. Sitting on a step with a crestfallen expression and pouting, he said, "I thought I was special!")

Today, these words seem trite or over the top, any remnant of wonder lost in repetition. But the incredible truth remains: You're a magnificent, one-of-a-kind image bearer of God. That we're each as unique as a snowflake is a fact, not just a cute idea for kids. It's an affirming and life-altering truth. Look at yourself the way God looks at you!

"How is that?"

From Scripture, here's what we see (try to read the words as if for the first time): You're a child of God (Galatians 3:26), an overcomer (Revelation 12:11), complete in Him (2 Timothy 3:17), in the palm of His hand (Isaiah 49:16), and His custom workmanship carefully stitched together, created "to do good works...prepared in advance for [you] to do" (Ephesians 2:10). You're not an accident. Like David, you were "knit...together in [your] mother's womb," "fearfully and wonderfully made" (Psalm 139:13-14).

You—yes, you!—are ultimately accountable to Him, under His authority, and purposefully designed as an uncommon laborer for the good work your Creator prepared in advance for you alone to do.

Let those words sink in.

May we never lose our awe and wonder! Even with our limited wits, these are mind-blowing truths to consider. And the more you focus on these certainties today, the less desire you'll have to dwell on uncertainty about what you'll be doing tomorrow.

"This is true for all believers?"

Yes. Let me tell you about Eric Liddell.

The film *Chariots of Fire* is based on the true story of two British athletes preparing for and competing in the 1924 Summer Olympics. One athlete, Liddell, qualified to be part of the team. When he discovered that his qualifying heat for the 100 meters, his signature race, was scheduled for a Sunday, he faced an issue of conscience. Given his interpretation of the fourth commandment, to "cease" and keep the Sabbath holy, he decided against competing in the games.

This decision to give up his spot in the race rather than dishonor the Lord was surprisingly rewarded. His teammate, who had already won an Olympic medal, selflessly offered to let Liddell take his place in the 400-meter dash, an event contested midweek. Gratefully, Liddell accepted, and he went on to win the race and a gold medal, setting an Olympic record in the process.

What stands out about Liddell are his faith and appreciation for divine design. Often quoted, he said, "I believe God made me for a purpose, but He also made me fast! And when I run I feel His pleasure."

Yes, your intentional uniqueness is central to God's plan. And your personal thread is part of His flawless fabric and greater story.

It's true.

"It's just hard to get your head around it."

Consider Kelvyn Koning, a music composition major at a college near me. Often, you'll find him delivering a piano concerto or writing an original song. He said, "When they hear the music, they're hearing the Creator's work that's taking place through His creation…I have a very real sense that this is what I was made to do. And I can glorify Him with this, and He loves it, and He loves me."[1]

And have you heard of Katie Davis Majors? She founded Amazima Ministries with a mission to live out the love of Jesus by educating and empowering the people of Uganda and the communities it serves. She said, "I am blown away that my God, who could do all of this by Himself, would choose to let me be a little part of it."[2]

I'm sure you've heard of the Catholic nun and missionary Mother Teresa. After 20 years as a nun and schoolteacher, she started the Missionaries of Charity. She wrote, "Each of us is merely a small instrument. When you look at the inner workings of electrical things, often you see small and big wires, new and old, cheap and expensive lined up. Until the current passes through them there will be no light. That wire is you and me. The current is God."[3]

Yes, while the Lord of lords could have done it all alone, instead He chose to involve Eric Liddell, Kelvyn Koning, Katie Davis Majors, Mother Teresa, and you in His work. Never fail to see the truth about your labor: Each day, you're a vital worker in a workplace that's illuminated by none other than the eternal Light of the World.

Here are some verses to remind you of your place in this detailed mosaic:

- "Just as a body, though one, has many parts, but all its many parts form one body, so it is with Christ" (1 Corinthians 12:12).

- "Just as each of us has one body with many members, and these members do not all have the same function, so in Christ we, though many, form one body, and each member belongs to all the others" (Romans 12:4-5).

- "As it is, there are many parts, but one body" (1 Corinthians 12:20).

- "Now you are the body of Christ, and each one of you is a part of it" (1 Corinthians 12:27).

Now, here's a challenge in a question: What if you lived out each day at work knowing that the Creator of the universe wired you so uniquely that we'd all feel the loss without your participation?

"That is challenging."

It is. And here's more. Before you took your first step, God prepared your broad path. He calls you to serve Him in the place where you can best fulfill His purposes. As mentioned earlier, you've been preciously chosen, divinely anointed, strategically placed, and fully empowered to work with God. You were created with unique gifts for this time and place.

We read the following in the Bible:

- "Now to each one the manifestation of the Spirit is given for the common good" (1 Corinthians 12:7).

- "Kindle afresh the gift of God which is in you" (2 Timothy 1:6 NASB).

- "Whoever serves is to do so as one who is serving by the strength which God supplies" (1 Peter 4:11 NASB).

In Jesus's parable of the bags of gold (called *talents* in some Bible translations), we also learn that God gives us work to do according to our unique ability (Matthew 25:15). We'll talk about that parable later as well.

"So God not only calls us to faith. He calls us to work."

Yes. His calling is to faith and to the work He gives you. Whether or not you realize it, you have a vocational calling. Everyone does.

Several hundred years back, from the viewpoint of the big thinkers, a calling was limited to a bishop, priest, monk, or nun. These religious workers devoted to the service of God alone personified "the perfect form of the Christian life" according to Eusebius, a theologian in the fourth century.[4]

"What about other workers?"

Eusebius thought that others (farmers, shopkeepers, and tradesmen), tainted by physical labor, could achieve only a "secondary grade of piety."[5]

"Tainted by physical labor? Ouch."

Thus, church work was elevated as more spiritual and important than the supposed "active work." In a sense, the "sacred" jobs were assigned first-class seats while the alleged "secular" jobs were relegated behind the curtain to coach. (Interestingly, until the Second Vatican Council of 1962–1965, the church reinforced the medieval understanding of a hierarchy of callings. One catechism illustration shows a married couple with the caption "good" and a priest and nun with the caption "better."[6])

This harsh view of manual work was held in the West until the fifteenth century. It was during this time—a bridge between the "Middle Ages" and modern history—that the prevailing attitude about work experienced a total makeover outside the church. According to influential Renaissance scholars with followers, we weren't to become like God through mere thinking but rather through productive activity.

Then, in sixteenth-century Europe, during the years of the Protestant Reformation, Martin Luther—a monk and professor of theology—went old-school viral when declaring that a calling was extended to all "active" or "secular" work, including—hold on, let me check the official jobs list—ah yes, even a carpenter.

As a result, any work could be done equally for God's glory.

Unlike the Renaissance scholars, Luther believed that a person was saved by God's grace and not by works. Also, he challenged others to serve their neighbors wherever God placed them. And according to him, a vocation was the specific call to love one's neighbor through earthly duties. He said God continues His creative activity in this world through the work of our hands.

To underscore his belief, Luther shared a hard-to-shake visual. He claimed that God even milks the cows through those called to do that work.[7]

"That's weird to think about."

And he didn't stop there. He also shared, "When a father goes ahead and washes diapers or performs some other mean task for a child…God, with all His angels and creatures, is smiling—not because that father is washing diapers, but because he is doing so in Christian faith."[8]

"God smiles when a believer changes a diaper?"

Sure. I'd say God smiles, so to speak. Because with the right purpose, all work is pleasing to Him—including changing a dirty diaper.

"That's hard to imagine, but all right. And no one has a bigger smile than a baby."

Maybe so!

Less than one hundred years ago, A. W. Tozer wrote, "It is not what a man does that determines whether his work is sacred or secular, it is why he does it. The motive is everything. Let a man sanctify the Lord God in his heart and he can thereafter do no common act."[9]

So why do you do what you do? What is your *why?*

"Help me on this."

For clarity, think about your work this way: God isn't as concerned with what you do—as all work is divine and service in action—as He is with why you do it. In all of your tasks, your work begins with ultimate purpose.

Your *why* goes well before what you do, where you labor, and how and when you work. Thus, ask yourself right now, in response to God's calling, *What's my why?*

Are you in your first job now? If not, do you remember it?

My first dive into paid employment was as a dock boy at a marina and convenience store. The surroundings were lovely. For these few summer months, my calling was marked by this spot. I helped the boaters and worked in the retail store. Although I don't recall the exact year of this dock-boy job, I know it came after the fall in Genesis 3:17—because, with sweat across my brow, I also cleaned toilets and did "pump outs" of boat-contained human excrement.

You'd be spot-on if you said I struggled to see these literally crappy tasks as having any worthiness. Looking back, at the time I may have chuckled if someone mentioned Pastor Charles Spurgeon's teaching—the "deliciousness of work,"[10] or told me to view my labor as service to God and my neighbor. (For more about addressing work that's not so pleasant, see *A* under "Chapter 4: Your Why" in Going Deeper.)

Hey, it's not easy to see the point of it all and to open your mind to the "theology of work" when you're trying your best not to breathe through your nose. This unpleasant work was inspired, though, no matter how unsanitary.

At times like this, and in the absence of floral-scented air freshener, it's helpful to know that a calling is the work to which God calls you. He initiates this direct demand and communication.

"That probably explains why it's a calling and not a choosing."

Sure, and you have a vocational calling, an invitation—and likely several in your lifetime—to work with Him in His kingdom. But only because you have an all-knowing God who leads and calls.

Being a dock boy and doing pump outs in air that reeked was God's plan for me at that time. I learned the old-fashioned way that, although work is good, some working conditions aren't so good. (For more insights on calling and work, see *B* under "Chapter 4: Your Why" in Going Deeper.)

So what should *you* be doing right now? Taking a cue from the wise men, if you're directed to follow a bright star (Matthew 2:7-8), be sure to do that. And if a radiant hand appears and writes a personalized message on a plaster wall (Daniel 5:5), get up and get moving. Pack your bags and your toothbrush right away!

All that aside, think less about celestial dictations and hair-raising revelations. Your calling response isn't over a rainbow or through the woods. And gaining clarity doesn't require an isolated intellectual or monastic-type experience either.

Interestingly, Frederick Buechner thought finding your vocation was less about grand moments of discovery and more about a "habit of awareness." He wrote, "Listen to your life. See it for the fathomless mystery it is."[11] Similarly, hymn writer Charles Wesley penned, "Forth in Thy name, O Lord, I go, my daily labor to pursue; Thee, only Thee, resolved to know in all I think or speak or do." Others describe a calling as experienced by a "secret voice" by which God whispers to the depths of the soul.[12]

But to each of those men I say, to find our calling, rather than from a secret voice or fathomless mystery, we can simply think here and think now. A call from God was never intended to be a riddle followed with a guess. So put away the secret decoder pin and look down at your feet. Rather than depending on a hack, trick, or fathomless mystery, *coram Deo* (i.e., being in the presence of God with all work)—continue to be open and available before God. And for today? With a dose of practicality, confidently respond to your Creator in your tasks right now. Your calling response is the work you'll do today, not the work you'll do someday. And your ten toes mark your vital spot.

Years ago, actor Charlie Chaplin said, "Look up to the sky. You'll never find rainbows if you're looking down." That's solid advice if you're an avid rainbow hunter, but I'll say it again: If you want to understand your vocational calling as a believer, look down at your feet. And there, right where you are, consider your work and how and *why* you do it. Where your feet are, so, too, is your response to God's calling.

If you've been a sky watcher, trying to discover your calling, check out a good story about late evangelist Billy Graham in *C* under "Chapter 4: Your Why" in Going Deeper. But have you ever looked at work this way before? By looking at your feet?

Yes, it sounds perplexing to most people, but your work—or vocation—is a response to join the King above all kings in His work right now. And rather than struggling to decode a divine calling, just remember to live in yours daily.

"Okay."

Martin Luther had a quick discussion with a man who had recently become a believer. The man wanted to be sure to glorify God, so he asked Luther, "What should I do now?"

Luther asked him, "What's your work now?"

"I'm a shoemaker."

"Then make a good shoe and sell it at a fair price."

In this conversation, Luther asked the man to fulfill his work as a shoemaker—right then and there—with a God-glorifying motive and standard. Whether you're a shoemaker, dock boy, or pediatric nurse, complete value has been tenderly tacked right into the labor itself.

So what's your response to God's calling?

Don't wait for tomorrow. Quit searching for something "out there." And for dreamers, put a stop to those escapist wanderings for the work not yet attained. Rather than more twinkly nocturnal views for clues, simply be obedient where God has placed you. That can be your why. Because God placed you where you are.

In Genesis 22, when God commands Abraham to sacrifice his son, Abraham's calling response is, "Here I am." In this scriptural example, he's prepared to accept the call before even hearing what God will demand of him. See Isaiah 6:8, where the prophet Isaiah does the same thing. "Here I am" is spoken by other biblical heroes of the faith as well—and by the preincarnate Lord Jesus Christ (Psalm 40:7 with Hebrews 10:7-9).

With readiness, then, say, "Lord, here I am!" Not for another place but at this place. Not with some other job but with this job. Not in some other time but in this time. As His one-of-a-kind image bearer and as part of a worldwide body of believers, the answer to your question—*What's my why?*—is in your immediate tasks and how and why you do them.

All God-glorifying work in your hands is ministry. Martin Luther referred to this as the "priesthood of all believers." He added, "Seemingly secular works are a worship of God and an obedience well pleasing to God."[13]

Today, as was true then, your labor is an extension of Jesus Christ's earthly ministry as well as the ministry He called His original disciples to do.[14]

FURTHER REFLECTION AND APPLICATION

What is the calling response of a first-year seminary student? What is the calling response of an aspiring actor who's waiting tables in a café? And what's the calling response of a dreamer who's currently between jobs?

As you consider these questions, remember that your work—whatever it is—is a response to God's call to join Him in His work not tomorrow but today. He is your why.

Ponder the following words from Nixon Waterman in his hymn, "What Have We Done Today?"

> We shall do so much in the years to come,
> But what have we done today?
> We shall give our gold in a princely sum,
> But what did we give today?
> We shall lift the heart, and dry the tear,
> We shall plant a hope in the place of fear,
> We shall speak the words of love and cheer,
> But what did we speak today?
>
> We shall be so kind in the after-while,
> But have we been today?
> We shall bring to each lonely life a smile,
> But what have we brought today?
> We shall give to truth a grander birth,
> And to steadfast faith a deeper worth,
> We shall feed the hungering souls of earth,
> But whom have we fed today?
>
> We shall reap such joys in the by and by,
> But what have we sown today?
> We shall build us mansions in the sky,
> But what have we built today?
> 'Tis sweet in the idle dreams to bask,
> But here and now do we do our task?
> Yes, this is the thing our souls must ask—
> What have we done today?

SMART-WITH-HEART ACTIONS

everal hundred different occupations and literally billions of jobs exist in this world. Right now, you may have a clear sense of what to do for a job or career. On the other hand, even if you're working, you may have no clue. And if you don't, you're not alone.

"Yeah, I haven't the slightest idea. This all feels like a test I didn't study for. And if it sounds like I'm confused…well, it's because I am."

I'm sorry to hear that. You might want to read about a time I was confused too. (See *A* under "Chapter 5: Smart-with-Heart Actions" in Going Deeper.)

Then again, being confused is okay!

Are you open to some help?

"Can you help?"

Yeah, I can. This is a question I've addressed nearly every day of my adult working life. As part of my career, for some credibility, I've designed psychological assessment tests completed by tens of millions of job seekers around the globe to screen them into the right jobs.

Let me introduce you to seven powerful and clarifying smart-with-heart actions.

I. REALIZE YOU CAN'T PLEASE EVERYONE.

Trying to please others is a losing battle. You can't please everyone—so (please) don't even try.

Each day, you may try to please others with your smaller decisions—such as whether you'll treat a friend to gelato, frozen yogurt, or ice cream. But you'll have an absolute mess on your hands if you seek to please others with bigger decisions—such as what your next job or career path will be.

Complicating matters, the deceiver will plant these kinds of taunts in your head:

That career? What would your family think?

That job? What would your friends say if you do that?

You know to get respect, you need a professional job that pays, right?

When I was a junior in college, after bouncing around for a bit, I eagerly shared with others that I planned to major in psychology. To this day, I remember the punch-in-the-gut responses:

"Are you serious? Really?"

"What are you going to do with a major like that?"

My head spun, and I was back on my heels. Can you relate to how I was feeling?

"Completely."

Do you have concerns or fears about what others might think—fears that separate you from God's call? Don't let them steer you down a different path. Though this appears to be an overly simple idea, it's precisely where most stumbles occur. Whose approval are you seeking? After all, the apostle Paul prompted us to ask ourselves, *Am I now trying to win the approval of human beings, or of God?* (Galatians 1:10).

Let me tell you about my brother-in-law's dad, Warren DeVos. It wasn't until he enrolled in the Florence Academy of Art at age 70 that he recalled a pivotal conversation he'd had with his father nearly 45 years earlier.

As a student at the University of Michigan's School of Architecture, DeVos took a drawing class. The professor told him he should be an artist. "I relayed that information to my father," DeVos recalled, "who told me, 'You can't be an artist; you'll starve. And anyway, artists are a bunch of Bohemians.'"

In the end, DeVos earned an engineering degree and joined his father-in-law in a manufacturing firm in New Jersey. He forgot the conversation with his father and focused on "being a good engineer." And after many decades and several assignments, DeVos retired and said goodbye to corporate life.

While discussing what to do next with his wife, she saw an article about why Florentines like to rent to Americans. She said, "Why don't we go there, and maybe you could attend an art school." Enthused, DeVos applied to the Florence Academy of Art. He was accepted, and for the next three years, he spent about seven hours a day taking instruction in classical realism with students 30 to 40 years younger than him.

Since finishing art school, DeVos has painted portraits of all his grandchildren. He also enjoys painting landscapes and still life. Several of these works hang in the homes of a prominent business titan. Others are in private homes across the country as well as in Europe.

His son, Bradley, has also become an artist, painting mostly murals. "Unlike my dad, I've encouraged him," DeVos said. "He does beautiful work." He added, "I think artistic ability is a gift from God. It's part of finding out who you really are. I believe that if you discover your gift and you diligently work at it, you'll be blessed in it, and you'll bless others."[1]

You won't please everyone all of the time. And despite your best efforts (and peculiar as it may sound), you'll even let yourself down. Please don't try to please everyone (including your parents) with your bigger decisions. If you have questions about that, consider Warren DeVos. After decades as a "detoured" engineer, with the right and godly perspective, he's an artist—a thriving artist at last.

2. CONNECT YOUR GOLD STARS.

Look at your life backward to discern your unique gifts.

Here's why: Behavioral science tells us that the best predictor of your future performance is often your past performance. That is, with your past as prelude, in rather vibrant and expectable ways, your prior years present your future days. (For insight about vocational guidance, check out *B* under "Chapter 5: Smart-with-Heart Actions" in Going Deeper.)

With that in mind, for this second smart-with-heart action, take prolonged time to flip through your memories. Dig out your faded blue and red ribbons. Find the pictures when your smile was widest. And recall when you were so caught up in an activity that you lost track of time.

Also, as part of discovery and recovery, reminisce about what came naturally. Remember when you received some obvious praise. List the experiences, unique skills, and hard-to-teach strengths, whatever they may be, that shone along the way. Inspired by childhood, we'll call these your "gold stars."

At a commencement speech, Steve Jobs, the late cofounder of Apple Inc., shared, "Of course it was impossible to connect the dots looking forward when I was in college. But it was very, very clear looking backward 10 years later…So you have to trust that the dots will somehow connect in your future…This approach has never let me down, and it has made all the difference in my life."[2]

"Is it all about the gold stars? I've been told to follow my passions."

No, it's not all about your gold stars. Author Malcolm Gladwell stated that "once a musician has enough ability to get into a top music school, the thing that distinguishes one performer from another is how hard he or she works. That's it. And what's more, the people at the very top don't work just harder or even much harder than everyone else. They work much, much harder."[3]

Your gold stars matter up to a point. Past a threshold, other things, such as your passions, start to matter more. And your answers to *Where can I help? What interests me?* and *What needs are most pressing?* will clarify your direction by design.

Your initial challenge with this is to connect your gold stars with what gets your blood pumping. Then find the overlap and never consider either alone.

"Why not?"

At times, you will find a link between your gold stars and your passions. Other times, unfortunately, the connection is broken. For example, you may have a dialed-up enthusiasm for playing sports. However, your unwilling, one-and-only body may be bad at sports. And have you watched auditions for talent shows? Some contestants are eager to inspire; others have this same desire…and don't.

To answer the *What should I do?* question, set aside plenty of time to find patterns of gold stars, and then take the advice of my high school career counselor: "Think about what you like to do. From this, identify what you really like to do. Then among this group of things, prayerfully consider what you really, really like to do."

3. EXPLORE YOUR PATTERNS OF PAIN.

Peek into your rearview mirror again. For more self-discovery, ask yourself these questions about when you were younger:

When did I struggle to keep up?

When did I frequently feel out of sorts?

Where did the doors seem heavier to open on the way in?

Write down a few of these memories because your earlier patterns of pain can direct you.

"These struggles are a guide?"

Yeah, and I'm not the first to say this. Charles F. Kettering, holder of nearly 200 patents and head of research at General Motors for more than 25 years, referred to failures—repeated failures—as useful "finger posts on the road to achievement."[4]

The Greek word *kairos* refers to moments when you're particularly full of God's presence and purpose. *Kairos* is the time when God the Father's calling is most keenly sensed.

It hasn't always been *kairos* for me.

When I was younger, my piano lessons didn't stick, and the annual recitals were a bore. In junior high, we returned my lightly used cornet trumpet much earlier than anticipated. In college, it was no real surprise that I didn't appreciate my music appreciation class. And after hearing my off-key singing to some gloomy number at a tryout, the decision-makers hastily cut me—no explanation required—from the oratorio choir.

My malaise didn't end with music. In high school, I skipped too many Spanish classes to count. Those dreaded linguistic lessons did much to help us memorize verb tenses and little to teach us how to converse—or perhaps they did, but I wasn't paying attention. Looking back, let's just say that the Spanish language and I didn't get along as well as hoped.

Today, it's no surprise that my calling response isn't as a bilingual music teacher. The frequent finger posts along my path pointed elsewhere. Looking back, although some of it surely stung at the time, I'm thankful (that last word wasn't easy to write!), yes thankful, for the repeated failures and caution signs along the way.

So what do your muddled, missed-the-mark moments share? Do you see patterns in your hurt, below average and never quite finished? Take some extended time to consider this. Run an honest thread through these aches and pains. Because like connecting the dots, the sharp shards from a shattered pane can tell a shared story.

Let's practice finding a pattern of pain. For example, consider if you've ever made statements like these:

- "I hated playing Monopoly when I was a kid. More often than not, I had more pink fives than beige hundreds. I sat at the table shelling out money, with my properties mortgaged, my thimble piece surrounded by friends' hotels, and needing to roll an 11 to survive."

- "In high school I flunked precalculus and, come to think about it, I never figured out most of the calculator functions. At the time, you could give me a month to do math homework, and I still wouldn't get it done until the night before."

- "Hey, I got some good news last week. I confirmed that I need only one math credit to get my certification, so I got that going for me, which is nice. Gotta say it, though. Another day passed, and I didn't use algebra once."

If you have made statements like these, it would appear you've been living on the left side of the mathematics bell curve for a while. So, then, you need to face your limitations and trust in God's one-of-a-kind, math-limited plan for you. And if you've been pursuing a career in finance, statistics, or engineering, at the very least, you need to pump the brakes. Really, you need to slow down and pray for wisdom.

Unfortunately, too often we fail to uncover these instructive patterns. We discount the recurring incompetence. It's as if we're afraid to admit that we don't like sand in our bathing suits or standing in line at the DMV. As a result, the world has crowds of uncaring caregivers, stylists without style, and salespeople who hate sales.

In a review of poor decision-making habits in their book *Decisive: How to Make Better Choices in Life and Work*, Chip and Dan Heath state,

> Career choices…are often abandoned or regretted. An American Bar Association survey found that 44% of lawyers would recommend that a young person not pursue a career in law…More than half of teachers quit their jobs within four years. In fact, one study in Philadelphia schools found that a teacher was almost two times more likely to drop out than a student.[5]

If you regret a career choice, at work you'll sometimes feel as hapless as a caved-in pumpkin in November. But when you do, let the truth about your botched efforts settle in. Rather than vacating the premises, ask, *What can I learn from these setbacks?* Because setbacks are never untreatable, though a repeated failure to learn from them may be.

In words attributed to Albert Einstein, "Everybody is a genius. But if you judge a fish by its ability to climb a tree, it will live its whole life believing that it is stupid."

Indeed, fish were expertly designed to swim. However, relative to a squirrel or monkey, even an earnest fish gets an *F* in tree climbing. Sure, thanks to this failing grade, the fish is temporarily in the dumps. But the fish, lacking any limbs or digits, can learn much from this failure. And if the fish posed the *I think I'm doomed— what should I do?* question, what would you recommend?

"Something in the aquatic field."

That's a great recommendation! Because no matter how clever the fish may be, even if it learns a nifty trick or two, it's still a survival-focused fish. Why strive to be a gill-bearing fish out of water, right?

Here's some encouraging news for you: Though you can't change your past, signs of *what not to do* (as well as of *what to do*) are all around you. God wants to bless you—and He wants you to know what He's created you to do.

If you think about it, after His attentive wiring, why wouldn't He?

Recently, I saw a church sign that read, *Dear yesterday, thanks for the tough lessons. Dear tomorrow, thanks for your patience—I'm ready now.* That's a concise sum-up of this backward-glancing, smart-with-heart action—explore your tough patterns of pain from the past. In the days ahead, be alert to the signs, do your best to see value in your less-than-amazing moments, and be confident in God's fully considered, guiding message.

4. JUMP INTO THE POOL.

Only 5 percent of people choose the right profession—one that truly fits—on their first try. Thus, the remaining 95 percent struggle as misfits. (To learn where this statistic came from and for sources to explore the idea of "fit" as it relates to generations, see some helpful sources in *C* under "Chapter 5: Smart-with-Heart Actions" in Going Deeper.)

Let me share why this statistic isn't surprising. In the history of major league baseball, only about 120 players have hit a home run in their first at bat. That's less than 1 percent of all players who have batted. And only four players have hit a grand slam—a home run with the bases loaded—in their first at bat.

As of this writing, Daniel Nava is the last player to hit a grand slam home run in his first major league at bat. Before the game, the team's radio broadcaster told him to swing as hard as he could on the first pitch because that would be the only first pitch in the majors he'd ever see. Nava did, and he hit the grand slam. He's only the fourth player in history to do so in his first at bat. He's only the second player to do so on the first pitch of his big-league career.

When it comes to your early work choices, you don't need to be Daniel Nava. You don't need to nail this on the front end!

"Well, I'd like to be in the 5 percent."

Yes, that would be great. But as with the kids from *Humans of New York* we discussed earlier, it's likely that, if you're in the early stages of figuring out your call to work, you won't become what you're planning to be. Even if you've been working for some time, you still might never be what you're currently planning to be. You'll need more tries.

But that's why the fourth action for you is *jump into the pool.* Take a deep breath and enjoy the journey, knowing that you don't have to figure out your next 10, 20, 30, even 40 years right now. Clarity in becoming what God intended you to be is often a natural by-product of time (and sometimes more time) and doing (and sometimes more doing).

Picture a scorching midsummer afternoon.

"Okay."

You're poolside, and earlier in the day, you agreed to teach a friend how to swim.

He's about your age, in good shape, and eager to learn. For whatever the reason, he just never learned to swim.

How would you teach him this skill?

Here's an approach: In the shallow end of the pool, introduce him to being in the water. Let him walk around until he feels safe and comfortable while you stay close by. With swimming, clarity about what to do often comes with just getting in there. The best way to learn to swim isn't by watching a video or reading the latest how-to manual. Nor is it all that helpful to talk incessantly about the topic. At some point, err on the side of action—jump in and get wet!

For your work, it's the same practical idea. Take the plunge (without plugging your nose) and welcome what comes next. If you don't yet have one, get a job, an internship, or an apprenticeship. And once you're there, hustle like you mean it. Chase the truth in a work setting and learn to work.

Believe me, it will do wonders for your discernment.

We can learn from an artist who dabs paint onto a canvas, but if it's not quite right, tries other colors and tones. When you're on the clock at work, fine-tuning, over time you'll have confidence that you'll gain clarity about what your loving Creator formed you to do.

For this smart-with-heart action to blossom, you may need to shed some pickiness and swallow some pride. You may need to cast off that often-present feeling that you deserve something better.

"Okay, but I want to figure this out and **then** *get the right job!"*

Now or later, go to *D* under "Chapter 5: Smart-with-Heart Actions" in Going Deeper. We have a lengthy discussion there about patience, and I mention some role models you won't want to miss. But have you heard the saying "Life is what happens while you're busy making plans"?

In time, your daily experience will be your toughest and most-respected teacher. And when the *It's not exactly what I'm looking for* job comes along, express your interest anyway. Then if you're hired, prepare to experience an honest day's labor—and pay your bills while you're at it.

"All right, but I don't want to take just any old job."

You don't have to take any job, but don't wait for the perfect one either. Here are two made-up but remarkably foolproof tips for searching for the perfect job:

1. Don't.

2. Ditto.

Someone has probably said to you, "Find a job you love to do, and you'll never work a day of your life." Though often repeated, it's more than wrong; it's completely unrealistic. Plain and simple, if you have a job without hassles, you don't have a job.

There is no perfect job.

You might find a near perfect sunset, Gala apple, or cup of coffee every now and then, but looking for a perfect job is a futile quest. As we saw in chapter 1, work in this world is no longer as sustaining as it was intended to be, and the friction between work as a blessing and curse is palpable at every site. Even if you're blessed with a "dream job," trial comes hand in hand with labor. You'll work with imperfect people and faulty systems because you live in a fallen world.

Can you have immensely fulfilling work? Absolutely. You're a part of God's amazing story of restoration at work. But perfect? No, the tedium-free labor ended a few thousand years before you got your Social Security number.

While we're at it, let's clear up another misconception: There's also no single "right job" out there for you.

"There's no single right job? You're killing me."

Well, there isn't.

So please don't start a search for the one-and-only "right job" as if there's only one per person. *This is the one!* thinking is doomed. It means if someone else gets the one-and-only job you're convinced should be yours (recall the reaction of David's brothers when he was anointed as the next king of Israel), then that person is in the wrong job—and so on, and so on, until every worker on our planet is affected like falling dominos.

When a job offer doesn't materialize, know that you've been designed for a number of occupations with various pathways to follow—and several of them would be good to have. (Let me also encourage you to consider shadowing someone who's on the job—a job you think might be good for you.)

When at work, you're a part of God's incredible process of refinement. That's why it's important to jump in there to begin with!

Just a heads-up: Sometimes this conforming or refining process is unexpectedly painful. *I hope this never happens to me* trials will come. And to achieve an indelible imprint, sometimes the Lord permits the despicable in order to achieve the incredible in you.

During the recent challenging economic times, I sometimes wondered if for every nonbeliever who was laid off, a refined believer was let go so the world could see the hope-filled, *no one can take my value* difference.

5. SEIZE THE SMALLER OPPORTUNITIES ALL AROUND YOU.

Each new day, you're presented with a potpourri of smaller opportunities. Seize a few of them. Unfortunately, we often fail to respond to them. Sometimes we decide about an opportunity by *not* making a decision. Other times, regrettably, we're just too busy, absentminded, or bullheaded to care.

Here's a rather practical example of a smaller opportunity: If a degree or certification is required to open a new door, and you're only a few credits short, get the degree. It won't make you any smarter, but it may remove a barrier.

Additionally, look for confirmatory insights in the little nudges rather than attention-grabbing flares. As David did, do a double take at undersized yet straightforward opportunities that come your way. His acceptance of a basic catering request led to a fighting chance and a victory of epic proportions.

Also, know that you'll often sense God's peace and general leading in the overlap of your passion, gold stars, and new opportunity. By new opportunity, I'm also referring to an apparent chance encounter, a casual discussion that catches your ear, or receiving the same advice from separate acquaintances. Consider the topical book that's sitting there, the intriguing situation that aligns with your prayer, or a job opening nonchalantly cited.

The opportunities and indicators range from the overly practical to the supernatural. The idea is to have your antennae up and be prepared to act. (Sometimes, however, God uses extraordinary circumstances to get His people to stop and listen.)

"How do I best find them?"

Read God's Word, as it never contradicts His will. Recall that Scripture has a lot to say about work. *Work* and related terms are mentioned more than 800 times in the Bible. Also, to hear God's voice, promptings, or suggestions with your inner ear, set an appointment—at a time and place when you're at your best—and prepare for an encounter.

"Set an appointment? Like at a restaurant?"

Sure, if that's a location that works best for you. And there, as part of an active two-way conversation, tune out other voices and tune in to the Wonderful Counselor alone.

But here's a big warning: With your preconceived ideas, concerns, and timing, what you'll hear may not seem logical, correct, or reassuring! But here's a promise: "If any of you lacks wisdom, you should ask God, who gives generously to all without finding fault, and it will be given to you" (James 1:5). Here's another promise: "In the same way, the Spirit helps us in our weakness. We do not know what we ought to pray for, but the Spirit himself intercedes for us through wordless groans" (Romans 8:26). And from Psalm 25:14, "The LORD confides in those who fear him; he makes his covenant known to them."

Next, if need be, ask others to share their wisdom with you. The Bible has many examples of people seeking wise counsel, including Mary (from Elizabeth), Ruth (from Naomi), Samuel (from Eli), David (from Jonathan), Ben (from Jerry), and the Queen of Sheba (from King Solomon). As we read, "In an abundance of counselors there is safety" (Proverbs 11:14 ESV).

slight pause

Okay, Ben and Jerry of ice cream fame aren't in Scripture, but you get the idea. And be sure to listen to a varied group of God's people—such as your pastor, teachers, or career counselors—who can provide encouragement, insights about your uniqueness, or even some accurate, up-to-date job information. And maybe, with their wisdom, you'll see your own behavior reflected in the actions of a frantic, shortsighted fly that bangs repeatedly at the inside hinge of a recently opened door.

By the way, for any opportunity, don't lose your bearings in the blinding glare of money. Mixing *What should I do?* with *How much will I make?* is a disruptive mistake. The trouble here isn't cartoon-like quicksand or animated sticks of dynamite. No, we're talking real hurt. I've seen the resulting damage hundreds of times. "The love of money is a root of all kinds of evil" (1 Timothy 6:10), and that desire for just a little more is a rich source of madness. Regrettably, most career decisions are a triumph of material hope over scriptural guidance.

6. TRUST GOD WITH ALL OUTCOMES— EVEN WHEN YOU DON'T UNDERSTAND THE WHY OF THEM.

God may bless you with a role where you're inspired. After a pillow-soft progression, you may have a job that provides services or products needed by others, generating something beautiful and worthwhile. During such a time, life and all that goes with it seem grand. As part of a summer symphony, morning has broken, the birds are chirping, and meadow flowers are in bloom.

But God doesn't guarantee such bliss.

Your Creator never promised you a job, let alone a decent-paying one. He doesn't ensure that you'll like what you do or do what you like. He never said He'd bond your passions with a job that pays the bills. And the Lord of lords never promised job security, an exhilarating journey, or anything of the sort.

Being blunt about this, what you vividly imagine, keenly desire, and enthusiastically act upon may never come to pass. And come to think of it, in your future, you may not dance in confetti, have even one shining moment, or enjoy a pocket full of change.

Life is not fair. (By the way, did you know King David had an older brother named Ozem? Though he's recalled by only a few, my guess is that his friends and family—sounding a tad British—called him "Awesome" no matter what he did. "That's Ozem!" Who said life was fair?)

Over the years, I've rubbed elbows with many people who started strong in a job but left looking like roadkill. For some, just trying to keep a job or gain a living wage—or experiencing having their work "owned" by someone else—in due course elbowed them to alienation. For others, the flattened end points of former grins now trend toward the floor.

Whistle while you work? Turn cartwheels across the floor? For some people, the cold brutality of a layoff, demotion, or reduction in hours was just another unwanted punch line in their story.

So are you off to an unsteady start? Are you staring at a paycheck amount with no comma? Or just wishing you had a paycheck of any kind to stare at?

Knowing all about humiliating ordeals, the Prince of Peace, shortly before His arrest by soldiers, said this for you as well as for every despondent, Depression-era Dust Bowl farmer years ago: "In this world you will have trouble. But take heart! I have overcome the world" (John 16:33). But Jesus didn't say anything like "In the unlikely event of turbulence…"

So though your job may be classified exempt by the Department of Labor, you're not exempt from distress, and you never will be. Jesus Himself told you to expect trouble and pain, but at the same time, ahead of sudden jolts in the workplace, don't let your ravaged emotions circle the drain. Instead, with hope, be ready for them!

Trust the Lord of the workplace with all outcomes even when you don't understand the why of them.

"Sometimes I think work is God's way of teaching us humility."

I think you're on to something there. And remember, the cause of your work story is how the King of kings uses you as part of His story to fulfill His purposes—not yours.

Now, to learn more about trusting God, let's get a close-up look at Joseph in the book of Genesis.

To call his career dramatic may be a disservice to drama. His winding odyssey begins at the bottom as his brothers toss him into a pit to die. In time, after he survives that, his siblings sell him to foreign traders and into slavery.

But oppression wasn't on his itinerary forever. Remarkably, Joseph rises to become the overseer of a wealthy Egyptian's household. And there—oh my, just when his life appears on track (and the birds are chirping)—Joseph is falsely accused of attempted rape and is thrown into Pharaoh's prison. Yet through an astounding turn of events, with the Lord's involvement, Joseph makes a comeback. He receives a pardon, enters Pharaoh's service, and rises to become the prime minister of Egypt.

Think about it: None of the disjointed details were predictable. At the same time, each of the stalls and turning points, both the ups and downs, lay completely in God's hands. Central to Joseph's life was the presence of God. As written, "The LORD was with Joseph and gave him success in whatever he did" (Genesis 39:23).

Roll the credits (again):

GOD

A helpful lesson from Joseph's story is to respond with unshakable obedience no matter the circumstance. As we see, God is much more concerned with the depth of your heart than with the height of your comfort. And to answer another aspect of your *What should I do?* question—though challenging to do—trust the Lord even when you're let go from a job, your dream is shattered, or you're totally thrown for a loop.

With no cherry on top, trusting God with all outcomes is your much-easier-said-than-done and sixth smart-with-heart action.

7. DECLARE DEPENDENCE.

Those closest to you can help with your basic what, where, and how questions. But even the wise can struggle with the "whys"—that is, the big insights to help make sense of it all.

We struggle for a good reason: Work has a fuzzy, ill-defined nature that sits squarely in the sphere of God's control and outside our control. As we read, "A man's steps are from the LORD; how then can man understand his way?" (Proverbs 20:24 ESV).

When I was in school, I asked my dad the *What should I do?* question. After a pause, he cited words written a few thousand years earlier by a wise son of a shepherd boy turned king of Israel. His name was Solomon, and he said, "Trust in the LORD with all your heart and lean not on your own understanding; in all your ways submit to him, and he will make your paths straight" (Proverbs 3:5-6).

After sharing this passage, Dad asked me, "With half of your heart?" But then he responded himself: "No, with all your heart."

"In some of your ways?" he continued. "No, in all your ways, grounded in obedience."

Looking back, I see that my dad sensed I wanted control over my life. I wanted to rely on my own smarts and chart my own path.

Let me be clear on this: I've never had control, and you've never had control. We'll never have it no matter what we do or how much we smile, schmooze, or attempt to buy our way. If it helps, watch a video of a 150-pound cowboy riding on a 2,000-pound Charbray bucking bull at a rodeo. When the massive, muscle-bound bull brings his rear way up…

Um, I'll stop there. I know you and our wide-eyed cowboy get the idea.

Has anyone ever asked you how the young musician got to the famous Carnegie Hall in Manhattan?

"Practice, practice, practice."

Yeah, that's the punch line to an old joke. It's similar in sentiment to, "You got this! Your future's what you make of it!"

But let's be clear about this: Your life is not, never has been, and never will be self-determined. It doesn't matter how resolute your plan, gritty your fight, or capable your steering. What happens next in your life is uncertain and is designed to stay that way. So dig into life's wider influences and claim, *I need help! I'm out of control!* Because you are, and so is everyone around you.

The book of James has a hard-to-miss comment on this age-old desire for control: "Now listen, you who say, 'Today or tomorrow we will go to this or that city, spend a year there, carry on business and make money.' Why, you do not even know what will happen tomorrow. What is your life? You are a mist that appears for a little while and then vanishes. Instead, you ought to say, 'If it is the Lord's will, we will live and do this or that.' As it is, you boast in your arrogant schemes. All such boasting is evil" (James 4:13-16).

The focus in these verses is a group of self-centered, type-A businesspeople. However, these same verses apply to your *What should I do?* question today. Here, we're reminded that it's not about our plans, fight, and steering. It's about aligning with our Creator's will. And while God is in control and upholds all things—big pause here—what you do and how you do it matters!

Sitting on your hands and saying *Nothing doing* isn't just lame; it's not a workable option.

"That's what I figured."

Timothy Keller stated, "There is a mysterious but real compatibility between God's sovereignty and what we do. On the one hand, we need to work, we need to do. We need to be as responsible as we possibly can. And if we are not responsible, there will be bad consequences. And yet over the whole thing, God is in charge of it. He's working everything out. You need to know both of those things."[6]

"What if God closes a door?"

Well, the Lord does that sometimes. Maybe what was behind the door wasn't meant for you. Commit to God whatever you do and be fully available to Him as you move along or…um, as you stay right there and possibly open it again in a fully obedient response. It's a door; that's how they're supposed to work. They open and they close.

David's wise son Solomon provided the summary instruction for this smart-with-heart action. He said, "Commit to the LORD whatever you do, and he will establish your plans" (Proverbs 16:3). If you're worried about tomorrow's challenges, consider these helpful words attributed to David: "Search me, God, and know my heart; test me and know my anxious thoughts. See if there is any offensive way in me, and lead me in the way everlasting" (Psalm 139:23-24).

Right now God is leaning in, and He awaits your declaration of dependence. Make no mistake, there's no co-leader in the clubhouse. And if you're piloting with the eternal King of angels as your passenger, wingman, or copilot, please stop what you're doing and switch seats with Him—immediately!

Are you ready? Because if you don't take this seventh action, taking the preceding six smart-with-heart actions will be worthless.

There you have it—seven ways to approach your *What should I do?* question. Nah, you're not lost, even with the many career options and jobs out there. Rather, you understand your calling response. You know who you are, who you work for, why you work—and that you have God's guidance in the chase for truth.

Now, apply these seven actions. And for each step on your path, be bold and have utmost confidence. From God's perspective, you're already *all ready*.

"How long do I have before it's too late?"

Who says it's ever too late? Are you feeling pressure to solve all this right away? Or have you been trying to figure out work for a long time and now you feel like it's too late? If so, remember that gaining clarity in becoming what God intends for you may take time—possibly a long time. And it's never too late. Don't forget about the retired millionaire who found his *What should I do?* answer in snowplowing, especially without charge, to some people who needed the help.

In a world with Sprint, Speedos, and microwaves, consider this: God does some of His best work when you wait actively. Jesus Christ spent about six times as many years as a craftsman as He did in public, itinerant (vocational) ministry. Pastor Tom Nelson states, "At first glance this doesn't seem to be a very strategic use of the Son of God's extraordinary gifts or His important messianic mission." Yet at His baptism, a voice of heaven affirms, "This is my beloved Son, with whom I am well pleased" (Matthew 3:17 ESV).[7]

—————— FURTHER REFLECTION AND APPLICATION ——————

Are you looking for more small opportunities? Here are some books that helped me with the *What should I do?* question:

- Bryan J. Dik and Ryan D. Duffy, *Make Your Job a Calling: How the Psychology of Vocation Can Change Your Life at Work* (West Conshohocken, PA: Templeton Press, 2012).

- John Van Sloten, *Every Job a Parable: What Walmart Greeters, Nurses, and Astronauts Tell Us about God* (Colorado Springs, CO: NavPress, 2017).

- Marcus Buckingham and Donald O. Clifton, *Now, Discover Your Strengths* (New York, NY: The Free Press, 2001).

- Richard N. Bolles, *What Color Is Your Parachute? 2020: A Practical Manual for Job-Hunters and Career-Changers* (New York, NY: Ten Speed Press, 2019).

- Beth Moore, *A Heart Like His—A Devotional Journal by Beth Moore* (Nashville, TN: Broadman & Holman Publishers, 2010).

- Tony Evans and Chrystal Evans Hurst, *Kingdom Woman: Embracing Your Purpose, Power, and Possibilities* (Carol Stream, IL: Tyndale House Publishers, 2015).

- Henry T. Blackaby and Norman C. Blackaby, *Called and Accountable: Discovering Your Place in God's Eternal Purpose* (Birmingham, AL: New Hope Publishers, 2012).

- Paul D. Tieger, Barbara Barron, and Kelly Tieger, *Do What You Are* (New York, NY: Little, Brown and Company, 2014).

- Marilyn Vancil, *Self to Lose—Self to Find: A Biblical Approach to the 9 Enneagram Types* (Enumclaw, WA: Redemption Press, 2016).

The book *Do What You Are* is based on the Myers-Briggs Type Indicator, the most widely used personality assessment. Separately, if you're working with a career counselor, ask about the Strong Interest Inventory or PathwayU powered by JobZology. Among countless assessments, based on lots of evidence and because I've spent a lot of time in this space, I'm confident you'll benefit from these.

Are you looking for more small opportunities? If you don't volunteer already, join roughly 25 percent of your country's citizens and donate your time with a group. These unpaid see-a-need-and-get-involved openings are all over the place. You'll find them waiting for you in your church, youth organizations, after-school programs, and your Lord knows where else. Start where you are, use what you've been given, and then simply do what you can. Helping with the smallest task, even when it's not tied to your talent or passion, can make a difference to those in need.

We see many scriptural examples of this action, and we're told that "God has given each of you a gift from his great variety of spiritual gifts. Use them well to serve one another" (1 Peter 4:10 NLT). So as a part of the 168 hours you're given each week, seize this smaller opportunity. Step out in faith and lighten someone's burden.

6

TAKING STEPS FORWARD

May I tell you a story?

A young man was rushed into an operating room at a nearby medical center. The congested streets of the city had made for slow travel to the hospital, even by ambulance, but the staff members at this multidisciplinary center were ready for his arrival.

His symptoms suggested a heart attack, and his voice had been emptied of strength. "How is this possible?" he whispered. He was surrounded by dizzying lights, state-of-the-art equipment, and the antiseptic echoes of unfamiliar voices. As unbelievable as it was, this myocardial-infarction nightmare was happening.

He'd been busy at work just one hour earlier, but now he was likely a goner in need of reprieve. In this grippingly intense moment, against the backdrop of a sterile palette, he was beginning to fade. *Oh Lord, I just need a miracle*, the young man pleaded. And in desperation, he tossed out a hasty *I'll do anything if I live* prayer.

Above the noise, the young man could hear some of what was said. He was relieved to be seen by someone others called "the great physician." And then and there, with holy competence, the Great Physician completed the evaluation, mapped the thoracic cavity, and delivered the needed care. And the young man, whose life had hung in the balance, gained the gift of another sunrise.

Fully recovered after a few weeks, without skipping a beat the young man picked up where he'd left off. Sadly, with renewed determination, he raced after

85

the barren wind, smitten by his swirling empire of dust. There was no end to his toil. And the Healer, who had always loved the man dearly, saw there was nothing to any of it.

Are you running after something you'll never really catch?

Solomon, King David's son (or someone else in the line of David), tossed out some water-in-your-face words about the outcome of a futile and prideful approach. His conclusion was, "Yet when I surveyed all that my hands had done and what I had toiled to achieve, everything was meaningless, a chasing after the wind; nothing was gained under the sun" (Ecclesiastes 2:11).

God has been looking at hearts since He created the first one. What did He see when He looked at King Saul's heart? Well, the general condition of Saul's heart was like that of this young man with the heart attack. Basically, when God—the Great Physician—beheld this first king of Israel, He saw a Grinch-like, hardened heart. It was not only the size of a closed fist; it clearly resembled one. Saul was a man after praise from others (1 Samuel 18:6-8), cruel (20:30-34), unforgiving (14:44), deceptive (15:10-31), fearful (17:11; 18:12), and separated from God (16:14). He was unstable and paranoid—and without much love.

And what did the Lord see in David's heart? Although David had many flaws, God declared the second king of Israel to be "a man after my own heart" (Acts 13:22).

"After God's heart?"

Reading this verse from Acts may cause you to slap your forehead if you're not careful. After all, David was no saint. He was the paparazzi's dream. For every Goliath in his life, there was a Bathsheba. For each person he showed love, he was responsible for killing many. But when David's life veered off course, God was undying in His mercy and love.

Remember, King David was always working, and the King of kings was always working on David.

Out of deep bruising and brokenness, David's foremost desire was to have a relationship with God. And amazingly, in time (see the very first sentence in the book of Matthew), Jesus is called the "Son of David."

Though David lived millennia before such things as biochips, gene editing, or cyber security existed, let's focus on one thing about him: He had a heart bent toward God. We can learn a lot by examining his God-honoring heart! So whether or not you have a stethoscope, please join me in taking a close look at three powerful qualities of David's heart: taking steps forward, embracing change, and being wholehearted. We'll explore the first one in this chapter.

For me, with some fear of heights, a short account from the Smithsonian begins to clarify this quality of taking steps.

Let's put a spotlight on a famous tightrope walker.

> During the winter of 1858, a 34-year-old French acrobat named Jean François Gravelet, better known as Monsieur Charles Blondin, traveled to Niagara Falls, hoping to become the first person to cross what was called the "boiling cataract"…A rope 1,300 feet long, two inches in diameter and made entirely of hemp would be the sole thing separating him from the roiling waters below…On the morning of June 30, 1859, about 25,000 thrill-seekers arrived by train and steamer and dispersed on the American or Canadian side of the falls, the latter said to have the better view.

The entire perilous walk—there and back again—took him 23 minutes to complete. And from that day forward, Blondin was known as the first person to cross Niagara Falls on a tightrope.

> After a brief rest, [Blondin] appeared on the Canadian end of the cable with [his manager] Harry Colcord clinging to his back. Blondin gave his manager the following instructions: "Harry…you are no longer Colcord, you are Blondin. Until I clear this place be a part of me, mind, body, and soul. If I sway, sway with me. Do not attempt to do any balancing yourself."[1]

In other words, *Let's do this together*—and they did!

Back to David and taking steps forward…if you could choose just one, what word or quality do you think best describes David's heart?

Based on the well-known Goliath story (plus a little vacation-Bible-school acumen if you have it), there's a good chance you thought of the words *bold*, *brave*, *courageous*, or something of the sort. Let's refer to this as taking steps forward when it takes guts to do so. David was bold (1 Samuel 17; 1 Chronicles 18). He repeatedly stepped ahead in obedience when others failed to do so. And as his faith in God grew, any failure to act because of fear withered away.

David's written words follow below.

- "Even though I walk through the darkest valley, I will fear no evil, for you are with me; your rod and your staff, they comfort me" (Psalm 23:4).

- "The LORD is my light and my salvation—whom shall I fear? The LORD is the stronghold of my life—of whom shall I be afraid?" (Psalm 27:1).

- "I lift up my eyes to the mountains—where does my help come from? My help comes from the LORD, the Maker of heaven and earth" (Psalm 121:1-2).

"What makes this quality of David's heart a big deal?"

Well, the all-knowing God makes this a big deal. This isn't a barely mentioned notion revealed only in small-font study notes for the book of Habakkuk. Not at all. For starters, do you know the one thing Jesus said more than any other in the Bible?

"Is it love your neighbor?"

No.

"Hmm, is it something else to do with love? Love those who aren't your neighbor?"

No, actually it's "Do not be afraid." Are you surprised? Variations of the phrase *Do not be afraid*, including *Do not fear*, appear more than 100 times in Scripture! God knows you and I need the repetition, and He knows any words about action in the face of fear are a whole lot easier for us to read in a library than heed in the darkest valley.

Although some of us refuse to admit it, we're all afraid of something. Every day brings the possibility of a new reason for alarm. That's why so many relate to the Cowardly Lion from the movie *The Wizard of Oz* when he confesses, "I hope my strength holds out." Beyond spiders and snakes (for some of us), we're afraid of certain people and things and unknowns in this world. But Scripture pushes us to move forward anyway.

- "Have I not commanded you? Be strong and courageous. Do not be frightened, and do not be dismayed, for the Lord your God is with you wherever you go" (Joshua 1:9 ESV).

- "Be strong and courageous. Do not fear or be in dread of them, for it is the Lord your God who goes with you. He will not leave you or forsake you" (Deuteronomy 31:6 ESV).

- "For God gave us a spirit not of fear but of power and love and self-control" (2 Timothy 1:7 ESV).

In case you haven't checked out the Catechism of the Catholic Church recently (just saying), courage is viewed as a gift of the Holy Spirit (CCC 1831), it's considered a cardinal virtue (CCC 1805), it's described as "to make strong, to hearten," and it's derived from the three-letter Latin word *cor*, which means "of the heart."

But here's the obvious obstacle in our workplace application: Employees are rarely required to display larger-than-life courage. Most workers never experience a *put it all on the line* heroic response. And few team members, spontaneously and with one shot, take an *of the heart* stand for virtue. So, then, no matter what your calling response is, it's unlikely that you'll ever be a hero at work. Absent any thrill-a-minute, popcorn-inhaling action scenes, I'm confident we can put away any slingshots, red spandex, and colorful superhero capes—even if you're a soldier, a medical professional, or a professional athlete.

In a *Harvard Business Review* article focused on the topic of courage, business professor Kathleen K. Reardon states, "Certainly, courage is sometimes a matter of life and death. Police officers and firefighters risked and lost their lives saving people on September 11, 2001; people dove into swirling waters to rescue strangers after a giant tsunami swept Indonesia in 2004. Yet in my 25 years of studying human behavior in organizations, I've discovered that courage in business seldom operates like this."[2]

In contrast to common portrayals of courage, the repeatable application of David's heart isn't a single step or an infrequent valiant act. Rather, with some anguish and trembling, taking steps forward is taking one step ahead and then taking added steps in the same direction.

"It sounds as if we're talking about doing and saying things that aren't easy to do and say every day."

Exactly! This quality of the heart is found in recurring instances and consistent actions—and the power is seen in the combined effect.

To appreciate stepping forward, picture a twisting, rushing river. With the passing of time, with etched grooves and carved patterns, the relentless river leaves an imprint on the hardened earth. And if you walk near it today or even several years from now, the visible banks are a reminder of where the determined river has been.

"Can you give me a few work examples?"

What do you fear at work?

Is it your boss or coworkers and what they might do to you?

If so, looking to David as an example, what's your next step? This habit demands that you walk with your head up and then face who and what you need to face today. Then face who and what tomorrow. And when progress seems dreadfully slow, this quality pushes you to tread where most fear to go—and then do it again the next day. And again the days after that.

So taking steps forward begins at the point where comfort ends, and it's maintained by your ongoing involvement. It's fair to say, given constant pressures on you to conform, that essentially, endless opportunities to transform exist.

"Ah, this is all fine and good for David, but…"

This is for you and me too! For example, laughing at what the new boss finds funny is easy. Scrambling to find something to wear for Hawaiian Shirt Day is rather easy. And enjoying a coworker's unremarkable birthday cake while leaning against a break room wall is easy too. But truly stepping forward each day isn't easy because it's basically an unpopular act of nonconformity compelled by God's love. And being an active Christ follower in the workplace is, well, sometimes, a step-by-step struggle…and battle.

"A battle?"

Yes, it's a spiritual battle and more. And because you know in your own heart that "the Lord is with me; he is my helper" (Psalm 118:7), this quality of David's heart demands that you repeatedly do what's right even when you're pushed to do what's wrong. Some days, with the knowledge that "the Lord your God himself will fight for you" (Deuteronomy 3:22) in the face of pressure or threats, this quality requires a clear yes and an intrepid, bold no.

At other times, knowing "so do not fear, for I am with you; do not be dismayed, for I am your God. I will strengthen you and help you" (Isaiah 41:10) encourages you to speak the truth in love.

So in matters small and large, fight to hold firm. Do your best to speak up. And be sure to reach out. It's easy to walk along with the crowd, but it takes guts to take steps alone. Yet you've been given endurance, faith, and guts for a reason: for good works at your worksite.

At times, unfortunately, you may be spectacularly unsuccessful in your steps. You'll trip on good intentions or say something wonderfully stupid. It happens! On occasion, then, you may step back before taking two steps forward. But, hey, it's still a good start. Your new three-step dance move aside, the exciting news is that you're ultimately moving in the right direction. Sometimes even the shortest strides are the foremost moves in your life. So go ahead. Take your time, start hesitantly, and tiptoe warily if you must, but be sure to take those crucial steps.

You may lean into this naturally or, more like me, you may be inclined to say, "Who me? You've got the wrong person!"

"Yeah, I'm not sure if I'm ready."

God knows you and what you face, and He declares, "Every place on which the sole of your foot treads, I have given it to you" (Joshua 1:3 NASB).

He knows you're the right person for the job and sees you through a clear lens of future victory. For any anxiety-provoking *Oh no!* moments in times ahead, you'll be given everything you need to reveal His power.

As seen in King David's life, the wise Lord of heaven won't always give you what you *think* you can handle at work, and that's certainly a good thing! Rather, God's Spirit will help you handle what you're given every time you go to work. *Every time.*

Remember, the workplace isn't for the faint of heart. But also remember who God chooses and uses, right? Throughout Scripture, what can you and I learn from the last and the least?

"God can use anyone, and He wants to use you...and me."

Right.

Let me tell you a tale about a guy named Carlos. Other than being rumpled and thin like a stray dog, not much stands out about him. He blends in with his surroundings, keeps to himself, and seems to prefer it that way. He arrives at the job site when most of the workers do, but he doesn't say much to anyone. He seems to be a loner.

About three months ago, Carlos's demeanor changed. He became angry, and he even got into a heated argument with his boss. In clipped bursts, threats and accusations flew. Thankfully, a few people on the floor stepped in to stop it, but although it could be coincidence, a couple of new hires who worked with him more closely have already quit. The orientation binder and coffee mug the last occupant had are still in the next cubicle.

Now, in more recent weeks, Carlos has been even more withdrawn. Unless addressed by name, he speaks less to his coworkers than ever. If asked, most of them would say they don't know much about him, but they assume he wants to be left alone, so they let him be.

If you worked there, would you reach out to this man? Would it be worth your while to do so? And do you think it would even matter in the grand scheme of things?

Wait. There's more. Carlos's high school sweetheart and adoring wife of 12 years has terminal cancer, and she's been given roughly one year to live. Since hearing the diagnosis three months back, he's kept this news to himself. So, with blisters on his heart no one can see, Carlos represents an opportunity for some neighborly love. The quality of taking steps forward demands that someone push into messiness and stay there for a while. Maybe God would want you to be that person.

Stating the obvious, God's workplace doesn't always introduce you to the people you want to meet, but many people with whom you interact each day carry weighty burdens. There's a whole lot of ache in the world, and your worksite is no exception. In their vehicles, home offices, or on a plant floor, many coworkers are connected as much by their sense of loss as by their aspirations.

"But don't most workers just look out for their own interests?"

Whew, that's a question tackled by Adam Smith in the eighteenth century. He's one of the influencers highlighted in Econ class because he wrote *The Wealth of Nations*, considered the first modern work of economics.

Rather cynically, Smith claimed that work is merely a means of fulfilling one's self-interest. He also suggested that no one acts out of benevolence but only out of concern for their own ambitions. He penned, "It is not from benevolence of the butcher, the brewer, or the baker that we expect our dinner, but from their regard to their own interest. We address ourselves not to their humanity but to their self-love."[3]

"Was he right?"

Unfortunately, when Smith wrote this rant, it appears he was surrounded by some bad apples—and he didn't give a hoot about any of them. However, it's fair to say that though many people do look out only for their own interests, clearly, many workers do not.

Here's a question for you to think about: If you're a construction worker, and you see a blind man walk toward an open manhole but you don't warn him, who's to blame when he falls in?

Here's a follow-up question: At your work today, what if a destitute, near-naked stranger crawled by on his hands and knees and pleaded with you for water, food, and clothing (see Matthew 25:35-36)?

This last one is an unlikely scenario, but what would you do? Because each week you will have many opportunities for goodness. They just won't be as obvious as our unclothed and unexpected visitor. To be ready, listen actively for hints of emptiness. In Christ, seek the voice of the excluded and devalued in your workplace. And while you're at it, with renewed purpose, be vigilant for strongholds of hatred and mentions of trouble nearby. Then take a step ahead, and then take added steps in the same direction.

Do not be afraid.

Do you believe in your heart that God, who loves you unconditionally, has a plan for you? Do you believe that you've been preciously chosen, divinely anointed, strategically placed, and fully empowered to work with God right where you are?

Yes or no?

Because if your answer is yes, your perspective and approach are forever changed.

Why did David take steps ahead while others held back? Did he dwell on his prior claims to fame? Did he throw caution to the wind to prove a point? Or did he rely on his confidence to get through?

Here's what he did: In obedience, he fixed his eyes on God and swayed with his Lord.

As we read in Psalm 3:1-6, with his power and royal status in danger, it was David's faith in God that allowed him to take many steps ahead rather than his strength or smarts. And with this same faith—though it's not easy—you can do and say what's not easy to do and say each day! So when your heart pounds and you want to walk the other way, remember this verse: "Be strong and courageous. Do not be afraid or terrified because of them, for the LORD your God goes with you; he will never leave you nor forsake you" (Deuteronomy 31:6).

"What if I just can't do it?"

I understand your question. After falling back in the face of a few recent opportunities myself—taking paths of least confrontation, the heels on my shoes regrettably worn from taking steps in the wrong direction—I, too, need to take more steps forward rather than just writing about stepping forward.

But here's my advice to you and me both: Tread into your workplace, the equivalent of riding in a wheelbarrow on a high wire (whatever your high wire is), because God is with you when you take steps of faith. And when you're run over by anxious thoughts and worries, call upon the ten words from the beginning of this book—*God can use anyone, and He wants to use you*—and tell fear *no*. It will listen.

God is greater, right?

But many times, your faith notwithstanding, you may still back down in times of threat. Take comfort in a crucified Messiah who didn't back down. And in workplace battles, you may not know the proper action to take, but, like David, trust the all-knowing God who does. You don't know what the future holds, but you can rely on the Prince of Peace who does know.

Right now, ask the One affectionately called "My Teacher" and "Rabbi" for a specific worksite assignment, okay? (Are you wondering how often Jesus was called "Teacher"—and why? Check out *C* under "Chapter 6: Taking Steps Forward" in Going Deeper.) And remember, the God who created the universe and makes the darkness tremble wants to use you to accomplish His purposes. The earth and His workplace have been waiting for you for a long time! Tomorrow and thereafter, across field and stream, by lot and carpeted way—so the world may know—leave footprints.

THE ONE AND LONELY

The following story comes from the *Detroit Free Press*.[4] Unlike our tale of Carlos, this story is true, and as you read this abbreviated account about a woman named Pia, consider the heart quality of taking steps forward.

Pia never married, but she was a sister to several siblings and had many nieces and nephews. Still, she seemed to be a loner. She rarely visited her family, and it was difficult for them to reach her in the state where she lived—even when one of her sisters died. The article in the *Detroit Free Press* says, "Some of her siblings tried to get in touch with her when they hadn't heard from her in a long time, but she often didn't answer her phone." One sister was quoted as saying she "figured that Pia was out of the country—or just didn't want to be bothered."

When Pia worked as a programmer in a technology company, according to a coworker there who became a friend, she was good at her job, and she saved her money. She also traveled extensively and had a nice home. But Pia didn't have a lot of friends at work. "She was just a very private person, and she didn't want a whole slew of people around," the friend said.

In 2008, Pia, having had a falling out with that friend years earlier, resigned from a later job after 23 years with that company. One sister said she'd heard Pia had an argument with her boss, and after resigning, she'd tried to get her job back but was rejected.

Pia made her last withdrawal from her substantial bank account less than a year later, and she seemed to have become more of a loner than ever—if she was even still in her home. But as the article explains, "Her life was so carefully regimented that things that could have set off alarms didn't—for years. Her lawn was mowed, her driveway was cleared of snow and many of her bills were paid automatically."

A neighbor Pia had hired to mow her grass and plow her driveway is quoted as saying in a written statement, "I continued to mow her grass because the effect of not doing so reflected negatively on the appearance of our lawn as well as our street and neighborhood." And when her mail stacked up, the neighbors told the mail carrier they thought Pia had moved away and that was why she hadn't taken in her mail.

In 2013, Pia's bank account finally emptied. No further automatic payments, including her mortgage payments, could be made. That led to the mortgage holder sending two repairmen to her house, now foreclosed, in 2014. They were the ones who found Pia. She was in her car in the garage—dressed—in a complete mummified state. She had died there five years earlier, cause undetermined. Her death was shrouded in mystery, and so was much of her life.

"She was a good person," her old friend said when interviewed by the article's reporter. "And it breaks my heart that her body sat there for so long with nobody knowing."

It appears that not a single person stepped forward when Pia—loner that she was—dropped completely out of sight. No one from her family, no one from her job, no one from her neighborhood.

Now that you've heard the tale about Carlos and this account about Pia, let me ask you this: Who's on your mind at work? And what are you going to do?

Because the One affectionately called Teacher has a specific worksite assignment waiting for you.

———— FURTHER REFLECTION AND APPLICATION ————

What are you afraid of or troubled by at work? Right now, choose one thing and then name it. Write it down and pray over it. Recall the one phrase Jesus said more than any other in the Bible: *Do not be afraid.*

For encouragement, read the first chapter of the book of Joshua and note the repeated, fourfold counsel to "be strong and courageous." Highlight verse 9: "Have I not commanded you? Be strong and courageous. Do not be frightened, and do not be dismayed, for the LORD your God is with you wherever you go" (ESV).

Fear of others? Or fear of God (a response of positive reverence; see Psalm 111:10; Proverbs 1:7; 19:23; and 1 John 4:17-18)?

Maybe now is a good time to make a choice.

7

EMBRACING CHANGE

Are you ready?

"Ready for what?"

The changing nature of work and your future. I'll tell you more as we go along. Given what's going on, it's important that we talk about it.

"Okay."

To begin, let me tell you just a little more about David.

According to Scripture, he was born in Bethlehem, known as the town of David (that's easy to remember!), in the territory of the tribe of Judah. He later fled to Ein Gedi and Ziklag and had royal residences in Hebron and Jerusalem. We read about him young and old and in prosperity and despair, often surrounded by chaos. David was a son, brother, father, friend, husband, seducer, fugitive, conqueror, and killer. His many roles included shepherd, musician, mercenary raider, army commander, and vassal of an enemy king. And if he wasn't busy enough, David solidified relations with various political and national groups through eight marriages. According to those who keep track of such things, David had more than 20 sons and at least one daughter.

"His life was wild!"

David was a change agent. He was certain to drive change as well as to embrace it. And no matter what you do, this second quality of David's heart—embracing change—applies directly, and with increasing relevance, to you and your work today. Like David, at times you may drive change and affect outcomes. More often, though, you're surrounded by adjustments and have little to no say in the matter.

Some change is good. Over the past century, we've seen advances in medicine and transportation of all kinds. But during this same time, some changes haven't been so good. Like powdered milk. That wasn't the best of ideas!

What wide-ranging change do you think affects the workplace the most right now?

"Well, there is a lot of change with technology."

For sure. And because of this change, some occupations will die, others will grow, and new ones will be created. Where advanced algorithms run free, jobs like parking lot attendant will disappear before our eyes. Other positions will be reconfigured beyond recognition. And what's "hot" these days will be modified, augmented, or possibly eliminated.

Martin Ford, a distinguished software entrepreneur, wrote, "It's a good bet that nearly all of us will be surprised by the progress that occurs in the coming years and decades. Those surprises won't be confined to the nature of the technical advances themselves: the impact that accelerating progress has on the job market and the overall economy is poised to defy much of the conventional wisdom about how technology and economics intertwine."

He added, "While lower-skill occupations will no doubt continue to be affected, a great many college-educated, white-collar workers are going to discover that their jobs, too, are squarely in the sights as software automation and predictive algorithms advance rapidly in capability."[1]

Jerry Kaplan, a widely-recognized technology innovator, stated, "Recent advances in robotics, perception, and machine learning, propelled by accelerating improvements in computer technology, are enabling a new generation of systems that rival or exceed human capabilities…Advances in information technology are already gutting industries and jobs at a furious clip, far faster than the labor markets can possibly adapt."

Furthermore, he said, "The skills required to do the available jobs are likely to evolve more quickly than workers can adapt without significant changes to how we train our workforce." He continued, "The nature of the jobs available will shift so rapidly that you may find your skills obsolete just when you thought you were starting to get ahead."[2]

According to the McKinsey Global Institute, automation technologies, including artificial intelligence and robotics, will generate stunning, breakthrough benefits for users, businesses, and economies. At the same time, for your worksite, the extent to which these technologies displace workers will depend on the pace of their development and adoption, economic growth, and growth in demand for work. Researchers estimate that 75 million to 375 million workers (3 to 14 percent of the global workforce) will need to switch occupational categories in the next ten years.[3]

And according to Cathy Davidson, codirector of the annual MacArthur Foundation Digital Media and Learning Competitions, 65 percent of today's grade school students will grow up to work in jobs that have not yet been invented.[4]

"Two in three kids will be doing work that hasn't been invented yet?"

Yeah. But even those of us much older should not underestimate the speed and magnitude of change. At some point, it's likely that you'll end up in a job or industry no one has heard of right now.

"That's crazy."

Summarizing research, Virginia Heffernan stated, "So Abigail won't be doing genetic counseling. Oliver won't be developing Android apps for currency traders or co-chairing Google's philanthropic division. Even those digital-age careers will be old hat. Maybe the grown-up Oliver and Abigail will program web-enabled barrettes or quilt with scraps of Berber tents. Or maybe they'll be plying a trade none of us old-timers will even recognize as work."[5]

"That's crazy too."

Many moons ago, there was a wise man named Heraclitus. He was a Greek philosopher known for his idea that change is central to our world. Heraclitus challenged the previously held notion that some things simply stay the same. He stated, "Everything changes and nothing stands still." And in conversations today, you hear, "Change is the only constant."

"Or, the only constant is change."

Related to these thoughts on change, have you heard of Moore's Law?

"Can you help me a little bit?"

Gordon E. Moore, the cofounder of Intel and Fairchild Semiconductor, shared ideas suggesting that computing speed will double roughly every two years or so. And his observation has proved true for at least the last half century. As anticipated, important measures of computing, such as processing speed, transistor density, and memory, have been doubling approximately every 18 to 24 months, which is an exponential pace.[6]

You may recognize this with your own—slightly excessive but no less brilliant—gadgets and possessions. For example, look at your phone. It has eight times as much memory as it did just three upgrades ago for pretty much the same cost.

To get your mind around the bigger impact of a consistent doubling in computer processing power, let's take an imaginary stroll. Picture walking along a country road for one minute at a five-mile-per-hour pace.

"Easy enough."

For a second minute, you'll need to hop on a two-wheel bike as you'll double your speed to ten miles per hour. And for the third minute, you'll probably need a powered vehicle of some type to double your speed again…and so on.

What's worth noting isn't just the doubling of speed but also the distance you've traveled. In the first minute of walking, you traveled a smidge over 400 feet. In the third minute, at 20 miles per hour, you covered nearly 2,000 feet. And in the fifth minute, zipping along at 80 miles per hour, feeling the wind in your hair, you drove a bit more than a mile.

If you double your speed 27 times—roughly the number of times computing power has doubled since the first integrated circuit—you'll be moving along at nearly 700 million miles per hour. And in that lone minute, keep your eyes on whatever's ahead, because you or your cosmic train will travel more than 11 million miles.

You'd have to travel to the moon and back about 22 times to cover that distance.

That's where information technology power stands relative to when the first integrated circuits appeared in the late 1950s.[7] And in pending years, future innovations will leverage this accumulated technology baseline. As a result, in seasons ahead, the rate of change will far exceed what you've come to know so far.

These days, already, technology developments make an impact on how we buy stuff, hail cabs, take classes, and listen to music. This same technology also affects nearly every aspect of work. And further game-changing advances in manufacturing, health care, and brainy networks are just around the corner.

I've seen the impact of this change while leading global human capital and technology consulting initiatives with some of the world's leading organizations, from ExxonMobil and Accenture to Alcoa and GlaxoSmithKline. In various forms and at different rates, this same change influences how work is done in medium- and smaller-sized work domains around the world.

When considering this, remember from earlier that every work sphere and sector—along with every bit and byte—belong to God every second, minute, hour, and day of the year.

Someday, on down the road, you may find yourself of sound(ish) mind, staring ahead with vacant stupidity, aware of a vast fissure between your need to work and your ability to do so. When that happens, take comfort in these words: "Even to your old age and gray hairs, I am he, I am he who will sustain you. I have made you and I will carry you; I will sustain you and I will rescue you" (Isaiah 46:4).

"Has your own career changed much?"

My career is an example of how quickly things change. Early on, my work emphasized measurement and statistics. Then my roles demanded expertise with organization design and succession planning. These days, my job centers on new regulations as well as advanced technical systems. A large chunk of what I do each day involves devices, systems, and mobility.

A few years back, I attended a conference in California hosted by a NASDAQ-listed software company that's an innovator in cloud technology. A privilege, this software company asked me to represent a client's perspective to industry analysts in attendance.

At the end of the session, I reflected on their questions. Each one pertained to a technology advance in just the past 18 months. Whew, the gap between having a strong sense of competence and a dreaded sense of idiocy is narrow! It's a fast-changing world, and at times I can feel quite unhinged in it.

"So how can I best prepare for a career where year 1 will only loosely resemble year 40?"

That's a really good question. To prepare for the future, let's check out what an ant, people around you, and David have to share.

"An ant?"

Yeah, let's start with what an ant has to say.

Daydream with me for a few moments. Put yourself smack-dab in the middle of a cool, spring day. The neighborhood kids are out in force on their skateboards and playthings. Not noticed by anyone except you, an inconsequential pile of dirt has pushed through a crack in the sidewalk.

It's the top of an ant colony.

Out of curiosity and some boredom, you walk over to take a closer look. To your surprise, an ant yells, "Hey, sluggard!" and leaves no time for a response. Then as she tidies up a small part of the sidewalk, upon much closer inspection, you see a "When in a fix, remember Proverbs 6:6" tattoo emblazoned on her leg.

As is possibly news to you, as a collective army, ants take boundless pride in ant-farm kits as well as being singled out among all bugs in Holy Scripture. Relative to the bee, flea, gnat, beetle, hornet, and caterpillar, the ant is the only insect recognized with a complimentary verse: "Go to the ant, thou sluggard; consider her ways, and be wise" (Proverbs 6:6 kjv).

The doggedly determined ant continues, "Because if you're a sluggard, we've been waiting on you for a very long time!"

You reply, "I'm not a sluggard. But I do have a question about work."

Without hesitation, the ant asks, "Did you heed the knowledge of the wisest man in Scripture and come for job advice? Because it's simple: Always consider the ways of the ant! That is—in any circumstance—be sure to plan, focus on what you can control, and hustle like the rent is due."

Is that the answer, then? We just need to work hard and hustle?

Well, it's hard to argue with King David's son Solomon, who wrote Proverbs 6:6.

"But I don't think that's nearly enough to prepare."

That's fair. All right. Let's move on from the ant and listen to what the people around you have to share. Your career counselor may say, encouraging you, "Take a few data-science and information technology classes even if it's not your major. And keep up with your certifications and continuing education credits."

Your mentor may state, "Do everything you can to stay up to speed on new work methods. You can't do today's job with yesterday's methods and be in business tomorrow." And, if you have an old man living next door, he may bellow, "Only a baby with a wet diaper likes change. Everyone else resists it. Don't be like everyone else!"

Already, emerging technology can outperform you and me in a wide arc of workplace activity. As a result—and as absurd as it sounds—your work will demand a higher level and different set of skills than your school was ever designed to teach. And to prepare for the future, learning professionals and career experts will encourage you to focus on experiences, not job titles or salary, and push yourself on skills like creativity, critical thinking, and digital literacy.

So did any of the preceding observations really strike a chord?

"Yes. It probably wouldn't hurt to take more IT classes."

During your career—given that you may have a job someday that hasn't yet been invented—how many additional courses will you need to take?

"A lot."

Yeah. And how many credits or skills-retraining certifications will you need if you'll complete work activities someday that haven't yet been seen?

Think about it: If ongoing learning and skill development are the key, will you ever have enough? And when does all this learning stop?

My guess is you know where I'm headed with this. Security is never found in more smarts, credentials, and learning—or in a workplace pension or retirement savings plan. So let me ask this: When it seems that every change in season, every variation in surroundings, and, seemingly, every quarter of the year produces some sort of adjustment, do you want certainty? And as you look ahead in your career, don't you want to put this craziness behind?

Let's get out our stethoscope again and take a close look at David's heart.

Even while surrounded by drastic change, running for his life, and hiding in a cave with a few hundred other men, David told the Lord, "My heart is confident in you, O God; my heart is confident. No wonder I can sing your praises!" (Psalm 57:7 NLT). Even in these most trying, chaos-filled spells, David's words are filled with hope and faith. And he affirms that his security hasn't changed no matter the circumstances. Yes, David gets to the heart of it.

And later in his psalms, we read the following:

- "The LORD is my rock, my fortress and my deliverer; my God is my rock, in whom I take refuge, my shield and the horn of my salvation, my stronghold" (Psalm 18:2).

- "Truly he is my rock and my salvation; he is my fortress, I will not be shaken" (Psalm 62:6).

Like David, ponder this in your heart: Sure, "things" change, but remember from earlier that all change is divinely guided. Everything belongs to God. Our world belongs to God, and your work belongs to God, and He is in your work. David says to God, "The heavens are yours, and yours also the earth; you founded the world and all that is in it" (Psalm 89:11).

And as we've already considered twice, every work domain—along with every bit and byte—belongs to Him every second, minute, hour, and day of the year.

The changes in this world and what's happening in the marketplace are not a threat. So whether you're a hopeful newbie or jaded old-timer, celebrate the changes around you. Have confidence that the Lord is in control of every small swing and oversized variation. Hey, the Lord was sovereign when our ancestors likely fretted about the future of the printing press or how the automobile might affect the horse industry, right?

And never forget that God establishes disruptive change around you in anticipation of transformative change within you. Transformative change within you is at the core of the gospel message.

So how should you respond to change and prepare for years ahead? Should you listen to an insect and the world's insights?

"Sure. Why not?"

Okay, pay attention to the advice but know that the ultimate action isn't to hustle, control what you can, or to keep learning with every chance you get. And the critical "must do" isn't to cling to what freezes, requires rebooting, or loses connection.

Rather than repeating "the only constant is change," ask, "What's the only constant in change?" Because at your work, know that the only constant in change is God, and your ultimate action at work is to embrace the change and abide in what's constant.

Pastor Charles Spurgeon wrote this about God many years ago:

> It is well for us that, amidst all the variableness of life, there is One whom change cannot affect; One whose heart can never alter, and on whose brow mutability can make no furrows. All things else have changed—all things are changing. The sun itself grows dim with age; the world is waxing old; the folding up of the worn-out vesture has commenced; the heavens and earth must soon pass away; they shall perish, they shall wax old as doth a garment; but there is One who only hath immortality, of whose years there is no end, and in whose person there is no change. The delight which the mariner feels, when, after having been tossed about for many a day, he steps again upon the solid shore, is the satisfaction of a Christian when, amidst all the changes of this troublous life, he rests the foot of his faith upon this truth, "I am the LORD, I change not" [citing Malachi 3:6 KJV].[8]

During your career, you'll see unprecedented changes in how work gets done. Count on it. And in the not-too-distant future, current technology will be discarded as useless, and the newer methods will be a trace of what they are today. We can all see where things are trending.

So I ask again: Are you ready? Because if you want to stay a step ahead, focus on an ant, your things, and behavior. But going forward, in response to radical love and if you want lasting peace and transformative change, depend on our Sovereign Lord.

Ultimately, the future of work is not about data or technology; it is the continued redemption of the divinely established workplace. And as turbulent air whirls about, know that alone, "Jesus Christ is the same yesterday and today and forever" (Hebrews 13:8). Certainly, in a world increasingly packed with dense circuitry, metallic hues, and matte finishes, great is His incredible promise that He changes not: "God, it seems you've been our home forever; long before the mountains were born, long before you brought earth itself to birth, from 'once upon a time' to 'kingdom come'—you are God" (Psalm 90:1-2 MSG).

Now, if you're ready, grab your new phone and that other stuff you bought, and let's get back to work.

THE PEER

Before a friend's funeral, I remember thinking, *We will go to your grave and say, "A great friend and peer has died. After many years, empty, he could give no more." But the angels above will celebrate you, saying, "A servant has been born and will worship our risen King forevermore."*

As you know, not all change in a work setting is tied to technology advancement. With that, let me tell you about someone I'll call the Peer for now.

Like me, Kirk pursued a doctoral degree in industrial-organizational psychology with an emphasis in statistical probability. Our schooling focused on the scientific study of people in the workplace. He had three children, and his daughter Danielle was his youngest.

A few decades back, Kirk came into our upstart human-capital consulting firm on the east side of Detroit for an interview. In my career, I've interviewed several thousand job candidates and screened candidates of all shapes and sizes for front-line to Fortune 500 C-suite positions. Rarely have I come away from an interview blown away, but I was that day.

For the next six years, we worked together as peers. Kirk was a pacesetter and difference-maker. He was also the first person I saw wear his faith on his sleeve at work. His presence affected the jokes told, the words expressed, and the excellence pursued.

Then I left for a position with PepsiCo/YUM! Brands in Louisville. In time, Kirk was a senior vice president for Aon, one of the leading consulting companies in the world.

In February 2007, he asked me to be a part of his facilitated panel at the upcoming Society for Industrial and Organizational Psychology conference in Manhattan. He suggested that we also bring our daughters with us. In early April, two months later, Kirk called me as I was cutting through an airport to catch a flight. The tone of his voice was different this time. He shared that he was having trouble with his balance and didn't know why. He closed our call by assuring me, "I'll see you in New York."

Later that month, I traveled to New York with my daughter. I recall arriving early to our session at the hotel, and I took a seat in the front of the room. Kirk was late, and the panel was to start in a few minutes. Then I saw Danielle pushing him into our meeting room in a wheelchair. He could no longer walk without assistance. I was stunned, and my world was changed.

I'm still not sure what I said to those gathered for our session. And at the close of the conference, as we said goodbye, I hugged my weakened friend as I'd never hugged a guy before. A few weeks later, Kirk and his wife, Angie, received a confirming diagnosis—he had ALS, also known as Lou Gehrig's disease.

After hearing this diagnosis, he said, "I really felt God saying to me, 'When your work is done, I'll take you. Not before and not after.' I have a peace to live for as many days as God has work for me to do."

Kirk died a few months later. At his funeral, I saw many believers (some from his witness) and not-yet-believers from his work life. Later, Angie told me, "Kirk saw all of life from the standpoint of his call to Christ. This view translated into integrity, high personal standards, and sharing his faith with individuals who often were people he knew through his work."

A few years before Kirk's death, I met his father, Ron. Ron was a Chief Judge of a 25-judge district and also the chair of Bible Study Fellowship in San Antonio, Texas. When I talked with him after Kirk's passing, he said, "God knows best for His kingdom and our good." He also relayed, "I'm sure Kirk had times when he was down, but he showed much good humor and lived life with all the physical capacity he had." He added, "That I would live and die so well."

From my closest work peer, I have a similar inspiration to this day: that surrounded by change, I would labor, live, and die so well. I pray for you, too, that "by his power he may bring to fruition your every desire for goodness and your every deed prompted by faith" (2 Thessalonians 1:11).

──────── FURTHER REFLECTION AND APPLICATION ────────

Other than the Lord, who is the most talented worker mentioned in the Bible? In Exodus 35, we're introduced to Bezalel, who holds this unofficial title. Regarding the design of the tabernacle, we read,

> Then Moses said to the Israelites, "See, the LORD has chosen Bezalel son of Uri, the son of Hur, of the tribe of Judah, and he has filled him with the Spirit of God, with wisdom, with understanding, with knowledge and with all kinds of skills—to make artistic designs for work in gold, silver and bronze, to cut and set stones, to work in wood and to engage in all kinds of artistic crafts. And he has given both him and Oholiab son of Ahisamak, of the tribe of Dan, the ability to teach others. He has filled them with skill to do all kinds of work as engravers, designers, embroiderers in blue, purple and scarlet yarn and fine linen, and weavers—all of them skilled workers and designers" (verses 30-35).

Years ago, how could Bezalel best prepare for the years ahead? And how must you prepare for a marketplace where two in three young people may do work that hasn't been invented yet? Let's learn from Bezalel, David, and Joseph's lives. To see overlap, please read again in verse 31, "He has filled [Bezalel] with the Spirit of God"; in 1 Samuel 18:14, "In everything [David] did he had great success, because the LORD was with him"; and in Genesis 39:23, "The LORD was with Joseph and gave him success in whatever he did."

Your current tasks are intended as an intimate partnership—with God's Spirit as your active co-laborer. And here's exciting news if you're feeling slighted relative to Bezalel and others: You've been given at least one spiritual gift (e.g., teaching, serving, or leadership).

Be thankful to your Savior for your gift or gifts! As we read in 1 Corinthians 7:7, "Each of you has your own gift from God; one has this gift, another has that."

BEING WHOLEHEARTED

Let's take a close look at what the third quality of David's heart—being wholehearted—can teach us about labor.

"All right."

David's adult life was marked by this quality, and no matter what your calling, this characteristic applies to you and your work. Forged over time, David had an intimate, wholehearted relationship with God.

Here are a few of his recorded words that spill over with devotion.

- "I will give thanks to you, LORD, with all my heart; I will tell of all your wonderful deeds. I will be glad and rejoice in you; I will sing the praises of your name, O Most High" (Psalm 9:1-2).

- "I love you, LORD, my strength" (Psalm 18:1).

- "I will extol the LORD at all times; his praise will always be on my lips" (Psalm 34:1).

- "How priceless is your unfailing love, O God!" (Psalm 36:7).

- "You, God, are my God, earnestly I seek you" (Psalm 63:1).

- "The LORD is my shepherd, I lack nothing" (Psalm 23:1).

He loved God!

Your relationship with God is the most important aspect of your work life. And when you say yes to His beloved calling and subsequent pursuit, you work in unison with God as Adam and Eve did before the fall. This is a personal invitation to intimacy—and your daily grind is a purposeful enabler of this bond. As Martin Luther said, "God's complete work is set in motion through vocation. He changes the world and he sheds his mercy on hard-pressed humanity."[1]

As mentioned earlier, the invitation is to leave your life and join God's handiwork. Each day the Great "I AM" calls you to purpose and confides, *I designed this work with you in mind! And I designed you with this work in mind!*

Perhaps you've never thought of your job this way.

Today, rather than respond, *Yes, speak for I'm listening,* many say no to God's invitation to marketplace intimacy. Basically, on their terms and with no obligation, they decline an unwanted call that's come at an inconvenient time. They turn *God's will be done through me* into *My will be done through God.* And because of this, they miss out on a hallowed relationship and God's design for them and their work.

Earlier in my career as an HR executive, I helped a Fortune 500 company president put personal belongings from his lavish corner office into a handful of moving boxes. Then with the help of a portable metal dolly, we rolled them to his Mercedes in the executive parking lot.

It was a Saturday afternoon. He'd been canned the day prior for inappropriate behavior—thinking no one would notice, he'd been exceedingly foolish at work. In the empty parking lot that day, I was witness to what it looks like when someone bottoms out. Then after he drove off with his boxes and trashed reputation, I removed all the framed photographs on the corporate walls that bore his handsome face.

This lunacy isn't limited to the corner office, though. A fall by a supposed bigwig just seems a bit more compelling.

Now, if you can, take a break from this book to read King David's words of lament about his own foolishness in Psalm 51. When it seems things are at their worst, when skies of blue turn gray, why we work is often most clear. In these gloomier moments, we see that work is a solution—until it's not. Unaccompanied, our work isn't the way, can't be the truth, and certainly won't be the life.

To sidestep this slipup, and to realize a surpassing sense of place, it's helpful to think of the workplace as a location where heaven and earth meet in physical space. And recall the Puzzle of Work from earlier—seeking you, God has promised to be with you wherever and whenever, the whole day through.

Fancy a blog post titled "Being Halfhearted Is a Killer!" The formidable stumbling blocks to intimacy with God are well-known. This slush-pile fare includes such things as the desire for more, an all-consuming pride in self, and being halfhearted. The parable of the rich fool (Luke 12:13-21) is soaked in the desire for more. And Scripture is clear about the danger of pride in self—the *I did it my way* mind-set. This attitude demands, *Give me the credit I deserve!*

To understand how being halfhearted is a killer, let's now dig into Jesus's parable of the bags of gold (Matthew 25:14-30). In the parable, prior to leaving on a journey, a master (representing God) delegates the management of his money to three servants. He gives five bags (one was equal to 6,000 days of wages for a day laborer) to one servant, two to a second, and one to a third.

By the time he returns, two purposeful servants have earned 100 percent returns. But a third servant—who hid his one bag of gold in the ground—has earned nothing. The master rewards the two making additional monies and punishes the lone servant who held no delusions of adequacy.

"The meaning of this goes beyond the handling of money, right?"

Yes. God has given each of us different (and often an unequal number of) gifts. And when they are unwrapped in His presence, He expects us to accept and then use these gifts in His service.

Here, the laggard servant wasn't condemned for failing to reach a five-bag goal. And no one pointed a menacing finger while yelling, "Well, that's a level of incompetence we've never seen before!" Rather, he was called wicked and lazy and thrown into darkness for doing next to nothing with what he'd been given.

He hadn't even tried.

"I'd say, 'You had one job!'"

In verses 24 and 25, you see that this halfhearted servant is afraid of the master: "Then the man who had received one bag of gold came. 'Master,' he said, 'I knew that you are a hard man, harvesting where you have not sown and gathering where you have not scattered seed. So I was afraid and went out and hid your gold in the ground. See, here is what belongs to you.'"

For most people, this parable is viewed through a lens of stewardship. That is, *What did you do with what you were given?* Basically, were these servants diligent in their work?

However, please don't miss the bigger takeaway: The one-bag servant squandered an opportunity to build a relationship with the master. And that's what the master wanted more than anything else!

In this story, this nameless servant's work investment ceased right after accepting the master's invitation. From the opening bell, he crafted a plan to fit his own wishes. And after a performance review, the master took his lone gift and gave it to the servant with five.

The sobering message is clear. Our Lord wants to live this life with you, to share in your days and decisions. He wants intimacy with you in the midst of delight and madness, in both the lasting memories and forgettable moments. In Jeremiah 29:13, the Lord says, "You will seek me and find me when you seek me with all your heart."

With your individual abilities and opportunities as a believer, to find your Lord (your master) and then to pursue Him even more at your job site is both a paradox of love and essential to why you work each day.

"I think I have some improving to do!"

We all do! Now, can you recall the master's reward for hard work?

"I hope he gave them a well-deserved break."

No, interestingly, the master's reward is the promise of more work.

"Well, that's a bummer!"

Not really. The blessing in the parable was increased responsibility, an opportunity to be faithful with even more, and more time alongside the master. And given strong interest in furthering these relationships, the master extends the invitation,

"Come and share your master's happiness!" (Matthew 25:21). In other words, he's very happy with his servant indeed!

As seen here, saying no to God's invitation foretells a bad ending, and being distant or ho-hum doesn't fly. The halfhearted servant turned his back on his blessing, his coworkers, and his loving master. He looked everywhere but the workplace for fulfillment.

Here's the problem with the rejected invitation: Work was designed as an intimate partnership, with God's Spirit as your active co-laborer.

Today's marketplace is overflowing with jargon, slogans, and clichés. And one catchy phrase is often repeated: "It's not what you know. It's who you know."

Can you guess where I'm going with this? Because it really is who you know that counts. And to ensure there's no confusion, the "who" isn't someone who can pull some strings, get you a pay raise, or land you a nice new gig.

Remember, in working out God's will on earth, you're in His holy presence, whether babysitting, creating a spreadsheet, or reading a book like this. Amazingly, before you started in your first job, God's Spirit was already at work for you, informing and shaping your labor. And now the hope is to move from working without God and working for God to working with God.

This big, on-the-job switch is the result of moving from a hollow sense of duty to—as with David and his God—a wholehearted, ongoing relationship. Don't hesitate. God will work with anyone, and right now He wants to work with you!

"This lifelong, five-days-a-week schedule is so much time."

You will spend more time with God at work than in any other place. You'll devote more time to work than to your leisure, family gatherings, and church meetings combined. Did you know that, with good health, about half of your heartbeats will occur while you're working? Between the ages of 21 and 65, if you work nine to five, you'll be clocked in for roughly 80,000 hours or about five million of your very best minutes.

Know that the Maker of each moment has an intense passion for you, every box on your calendar, and each of the roughly 300 million seconds He's potentially given to you for labor. So on and on you go. And I may have vastly underestimated the amount of time spent working since these numbers reflect only 40 hours (not 24/7 and "always on") for 40 years.

"Forty years. That's how long Moses and the Israelites wandered in the desert!"

Today, it seems we've merely replaced the complaints about manna, locusts, and honey with our grumbles about health care, taxes, and money. Whether surrounded by hot sand then or a sea of cubicles now, not that much has changed. And certainly, as believers in His marketplace, it's time to change that!

Hey, can we talk for a bit about our performance at work?

"Sure."

During your many work hours, finding freedom and joy comes from knowing and loving God. And the message of Jesus Christ, pinpointing God's grace, applies to everything you do. Jesus's emphasis, in glaring contrast to the political leaders as well as to the Sanhedrin and specifically the Pharisees, was not on works or credentials. Rather, we read, "The Son of Man came to seek and save the lost" (Luke 19:10).

"What are you saying? Does my performance even matter?"

This doesn't mean work quality is unimportant. Your teacher will give you a bad grade if you don't show you've grasped the material. A faith-driven athlete will be benched for crummy results. Halfhearted workers will be put on a Performance Improvement Plan when they tinker around, miss objectives, and get lost in some habits of idleness. And if your vacuum cleaner rolls over a piece of lint without picking it up, you'll bend down, pick up the lint, put it in front of your vacuum, and hope for a better result—but for only so long. Soon you'll start looking for a new vacuum. Agreed?

"So my work performance does matter."

It does. Especially when it's done wholeheartedly.

Let me share another family story.

When my wife was in second grade, as part of a school art project, her teacher had each student make a map holder for Father's Day. We're talking about a pouch-like container for those old-style, foldable paper maps. The map holder could be kept in a car's glove compartment.

My wife recalled,

> I remember not wanting to give my dad a gift made of plain paper. So, when I got home after school, I found scissors and a needle and yarn, gathered additional materials, and made a completely new holder out of purple felt. I meticulously stitched it together with colorful yarn and then cut an outline of a small car from yellow felt. After that, I delicately glued the yellow felt car onto the holder. To this day, I remember my dad's smile when I gave him this gift. He held my hand as we walked out to his car. He put his holder in his car's glove compartment, and then he filled it with his other local city maps. In the few years that followed, I loved being on trips and seeing him use it. I was glad I'd taken time to make a beautiful holder. I loved my dad! And I know he loved me for just being me. Even then, you know, I sensed he didn't need me to make the gift that special. I guess I just really wanted to give him my best.

As beautiful as her gift was in my wife's eyes, my father-in-law didn't need a map holder in the least, right? At the same time, with obvious symbolism, he loved his daughter and their time together, and he adored her effort. Author and speaker Jefferson Bethke wrote, "As image-bearers, our job is to be gardeners as Adam was before he ate the fruit. We are to take raw materials, make something creative and beautiful, and then offer that to God as worship."[2]

"That's nice and all, but what about my job performance?"

When you clock in or power up, your responsibility at work is to work. Years back, novelist and playwright Dorothy Sayers wrote the following.

> The church's approach to an intelligent carpenter is usually confined to exhorting him to not be drunk or disorderly in his leisure hours and to come to church on Sundays. What the church should be telling him is this: that the very first demand that his religion makes upon him is that he should make good tables.[3]

Although not always easy to do—recall my unsanitary tasks as a dock boy—respect the blessing of work you've received. And know that while your value to God isn't what you do, your excellence does matter—to your supervisor, to your coworkers, to every customer, and to others who count on you.

Stay close with me.

So with plenty of grit and lots of sweat, be holy because God is holy. And like David, in wholehearted submission, do your best to echo His awesome work. Whatever you do, in praise and as a grateful response…

Be a determined worker ("make good tables").	Why? To glorify Him.
Complete even the simplest tasks with care…	…as you **W**orship **O**ur **R**isen **K**ing.
Treat others better than they treat you.	Why? To love them and God.
Work enthusiastically…	"…for you know that nothing you do for the Lord is ever useless" (1 Corinthians 15:58 NLT).
Stand firm in your faith. Be available and vigilant…	…as His true and loyal servant.
In truth and for justice, stand for the truth.	Why? To emulate the Spirit of Truth and the One who said, "I am the way and the truth and the life" (John 14:6).
Do what's right even if it's easier to do what's wrong…	…to adore the One enthroned in heaven.
In humility, help others who can't help you…	…to be His hands and feet.
Take repeated steps forward.	Why? With joy, to honor the Most High.
Embrace change…	…and abide in the Lord of the workplace.
Place your work before God as a sacrificial offering. And then rest and play…	…to declare dependence on and delight in your Creator.

This is what the one and only worthy One desires, starting with giving Him glory! Pastor John Van Sloten said,

> What is it about any craftsperson, working with her hands, that often feels so right? Did God make this artisan to know him via touch, via her hands? People who work in the trades often talk about how they love working with their hands and how it comes naturally to them. And it should come naturally! God made those hands! He created our sense of touch as a means of engaging his revelation in a physical world. It is a different—but valid—way of knowing and worshiping.

He added the following,

> Surely Jesus knew that all of the physicality he embodied was a gift from God his Father (one that he would take back to his Father one day). He must have looked at his hands and marveled. Carpentry might have been a very spiritual discipline for him—every move a rite, each thought a word from God, every action communion.[4]

The connection between work and worship is revealed in the link between what you do (the work examples on the left side of the preceding list) and ultimately why you do it (the worship examples on the right side of the list).

Do you see why you've been called to work? The amazing *why* of work? It's right there!

Said more formally, the purpose of your work is found in the union of your occupation (the left side of the list) and your preoccupation with God (the right side of the list). And when you focus solely on your ability, what you do, and how you're doing, you miss the greatest, grace-filled opportunity—with its availability, offering your work as worship for God.

Let me ask, then, is it any surprise that in Hebrew, the words translated as *work*, *worship*, and *service* are derived from the same root word—*avodah*? And is it any wonder that the Bible bridges work and worship and presents both as a duty-free action aimed at service?

No matter your place, worship (what ascends from your heart to God) is not unique to praise songs, the church, praying, or the Sabbath. For His highest, your work and worship—yes, two words in a stormy relationship and thus rarely seen in the same sentence—are seamlessly sewn together. And in time—though you won't be able to keep your full and solemn attention on God amid workplace noises, pressures, and distractions—you'll experience the Lord as the union of your work, and worship blots out the prideful worship of work and what comes from it.

So rather than ever wondering if your work performance matters, here's a more important question to consider: What does God ask of you at work?

"Help me on this."

It's a considerable question, because God doesn't need anything from you. He's entirely complete apart from the most spectacular anything you'll ever do. God doesn't ask you to work for free. In response, before that final whistle blows, receive His sufficient gift of grace and work as free. You have absolutely nothing to prove.

That's what God asks of you at work!

A key text in our conversation has been "we are God's handiwork, created in Christ Jesus to do good works, which God prepared in advance for us to do" (Ephesians 2:10). In line with this, and shared in the same breath, are the two verses that precede it: "It is by grace you have been saved, through faith—and this is not from yourselves, it is the gift of God—not by works, so that no one can boast" (verses 8-9).

Do you struggle with a nagging need to prove yourself? Timothy Keller states the following:

> The gospel frees us from the relentless pressure of having to prove ourselves and secure our identity through work, for we are already proven and secure. It also frees us from a condescending attitude toward less sophisticated labor and from envy over more exalted work. All work now becomes a way to love the God who saved us freely; and by extension, a way to love our neighbor.[5]

As a servant of the living God, you're no longer bound by the question *Am I good enough?* because you can never be good enough no matter what you do.

"No matter what I do?"

No matter what you do.

Whether you're a schoolteacher, roadside sign twirler, or in the military, your identity can never be reduced to a title. Your job title and description can never be your self-description. And your identity can't be fused to failures or bonded to your successes.

The source of your identity isn't in a title, your performance, or what you've done, but in our God, who adopted you in Christ's name. As a child of God, you aren't who you are because of what you do; you're who you are because of whose you are.

Consider this truth the next time you introduce yourself: "Hi, my name is [your name here], and I'm a [your job here]."

It's not about your work legacy. It's not about your feats, goings-on, or zip code. And as a free gift, it's not about being more determined. No matter what you do or how hard you try—any acrylic trophies, standing ovations, or high fives for good works notwithstanding—somehow, it'll never do.

Like dandelion wisps of nothingness, the feel-good kudos and your tireless actions will never win our Deliverer's blessing. Never. Because by way of nails and rugged wood, a calloused craftsman from Galilee stood in the way of judgment and forever cut our claims, reset the calculations, and sanded off any labels.

So put the pride aside. Stop trying to earn "good enough"!

"In other words, I don't have to get it all because I already have it all?"

That's right! As a believer, after repentance, what's vital to having it all is understanding that you already do (John 6:28-29).

"And I don't need to worry about some kind of work legacy?"

Can you name your country's last five presidents or prime ministers? What did your grandfather's father or mother do for a living? And can you share anything about your grandfather's father's parents? If you struggled with your memory or just never have known, understand that "no one remembers the former generations, and even those yet to come will not be remembered by those who follow them" (Ecclesiastes 1:11).

The notion of leaving a work legacy is a funny thing. Even if you outpace the pack, make a name for yourself, labor selflessly in an orphanage, or unfortunately, do something woeful, your life and works will be forgotten.

So what does that say about a solid reputation, years spent in service, or a to-die-for epitaph? Scripture says, "All of us have become like one who is unclean, and all our righteous acts are like filthy rags; we all shrivel up like a leaf, and like the wind our sins sweep us away" (Isaiah 64:6). In this verse, the precise meaning of "filthy rags" is "menstrual garments." And if you're repulsed or unsettled by that, then Isaiah's words got the desired reaction. Because that's how any "good deeds" appear relative to your Creator's grace and holiness.

Do you need a pick-me-up? Stop that chase! Remember that you have nothing to prove. Your identity and purpose aren't found in your work or in anything that comes from it. Through Jesus the Christ, with liberating joy and thankfulness, you already have identity and purpose!

As a kid, I occasionally heard this simple song: "Happy, happy, happy, happy, I'm a happy young man. I work eight hours. I sleep eight hours and have eight hours of fun." Every now and then, someone in the family would sing that tune—usually, just because.

The song reminds me of words shared by my Dutch grandparents—survivors of war and the Great Depression—*werk maakt het leven zoet.* That is, *work makes life sweet.*

Work is good.

"It sounds like work's been good for you. Well, after that job with boats."

I've had a wide variety of paid jobs since I was that marina dock boy doing the occasional "pump-out." A line job at a pickle factory? Check. Janitorial cleaning with an ever-present mop bucket? Check. Minimum-wage dishwasher in a mall café? You got it. Food-prep crew member at Burger King? Been there. Sports instructor? Landscaper? Cutlery salesman? Classroom teacher? Traveling business consultant? Yes. An executive in Fortune 500 boardrooms? Done that too.

On occasion, I've experienced the direct effects of evil and slogged through them with cruel and mean-spirited people. At other times, I've labored shoulder to shoulder with inspiring and godly servants in unique and memorable spots.

I consider myself blessed through each of these various jobs. And although I still shy away from taking steps forward too often, I've seen the amazing power of taking steps forward. I've come to know the importance of embracing change. And I know in my head and heart that I can work with freedom when I am a whole-hearted follower of Jesus. The sun rose and the sun set. Though often difficult, these days were a blessing, and the work was more than a job.

But even on the good days, work isn't as sweet as it will be when we get to where we're going. As a believer, you've been promised gloriously renewed days ahead. You see, this world, and the vast marketplace in it—even though it's out of sync—is the forerunner of the new heaven and new earth, which will be perfectly puri-fied, restored, and enhanced.

All around you, God is actively working to prepare the world and the market-place in it for Jesus's return. The everlasting Father created the world, the Name above all names redeemed it, and at this minute, the Alpha and Omega is work-ing to sustain and remake it. The completion of God's victorious work is certain but not fully realized…yet.

Then we'll say *So long!* to the pink slips, missing red staplers, and infectiously ill people sneezing nearby. In this new creation, there won't be a single labor strike, graveyard shift, or prehire urine test. No more online job applications. No more emotional whiplash from the boss. Security badges, existing out of habit, and the repeated cycle of waiting for the weekend will be old memories. And when the rough becomes smooth, any suffering from chronic joblessness, barely hanging on, or not getting by at all will be a thing of the past.

Continuing with the good news…

When Jesus returns in strength, we'll have no weary commutes or indignities small but steady. And when the crooked is made straight, every laborer will shout *Goodbye!* to their fears, medications, and early-morning alarms. Although you might have to attend a long meeting or two just for old time's sake, get ready for an eternal celebration ahead!

Though we can't see the future, we do get to read about it.

In 2 Corinthians 4:17-18, in this paraphrase, we hear, "These hard times are small potatoes compared to the coming good times, the lavish celebration prepared for us. There's far more here than meets the eye. The things we see now are here today, gone tomorrow. But the things we can't see now will last forever" (MSG).

Here's what the apostle John recorded:

> Then I saw a new heaven and a new earth…And I heard a loud voice from the throne saying, "Look! God's dwelling place is now among the people, and he will dwell with them. They will be his people, and God himself will be with them and be their God. He will wipe every tear from their eyes. There will be no more death or mourning or crying or pain, for the old order of things has passed away." He who was seated on the throne said, "I am making everything new!" Then he said, "Write this down, for these words are trustworthy and true" (Revelation 21:1,3-5).

"It's hard to envision what's ahead."

It is! Heaven is so much greater than what our minds can imagine. It's hard enough to guess what work here will be in 40 years, right?

Conscious of heaven and thinking about eternity, no one knows for sure if the artists will finish their abandoned paintings someday. And nobody is certain what bodybuilders, life insurance salesmen, crime-scene investigators, and, sure, Halloween mask makers will do for service.

We read, "As it is written, Eye hath not seen, nor ear heard, neither have entered into the heart of man, the things which God hath prepared for them that love him" (1 Corinthians 2:9 KJV). Without decay, death, crime, sorrow, disability, and even those bad-hair days, blissful service will take on an eternal sin-free form and function we can only anticipate with hope.

If you're wondering if that means you'll work in heaven, we don't know everything this side of a starry, starry night, but understand that your call to glorify the everlasting God will never end.

In the old Westminster Shorter Catechism, the first question reads, "What is the chief end of man?" Though we are formed to work, work isn't our chief end at all. The answer states that our "chief end is to glorify God, and to enjoy him forever." And here's what's brain-boggling to consider: Both your ultimate purpose and God's invitation to intimacy apply to your labor today as well as to your "face-to-face" active service (Revelation 7:15; 22:3)—forevermore.

Oh Lord, oh Lord, our God.

I'm so excited for you!

The God who created the universe wants to use you to accomplish His purposes now. The earth and the workplace have been waiting for you for a very long time! Know that the ten words from the start of this book—*God can use anyone, and He wants to use you*—are true!

It seems like just yesterday that my younger son was three years old, in the bathtub and surrounded by a mound of newly stirred-up bubbles. When I told him it was time to get out, he replied, "But I'm not done working yet, Dad."

Now, at the time, he didn't really understand what work was—let alone who he was or who God is. Here, with *Work Worth Doing*, I pray I've helped each of my children and you, my readers, to answer many common work questions, and to connect the dots between our God, the worthiness of work, and who you're meant to be.

Thankfully, God didn't wait until your hair was gray, your bottom was wide, and your last task was finished to express His love to you. Rather, your Lord announced, *Well done, My child!* at the beginning of your relationship.

And let's not complicate things, because we don't need to. *Jesus loves me, this I know, for the Bible tells me so.* Agreed? Your relationship with God is the most important thing at work. Now simply respond to His invitation of intimacy at work, and wholeheartedly love your heavenly Father right back (Romans 10:9-10).

As I said up front, on one hand, this extended letter of a book is about work, but on the other hand, it's not about work at all. It's about your work only in the context of something far more important—your life and eternity. And in the years ahead, as you anticipate the imminent blank pages in your own work story, may our God take away your breath with wonder, fill your eyes with tears because of His love, and share intimately with you in even the most menial of tasks.

Your work story and His work story don't end here. As God has blessed you with work, may you now bless and uplift others with what you do. When our Creator looked right at you and the fruit of His labor, He saw enduring beauty and declared, *It is very good!*

Roll the credits (again)…

GOD

THE TEACHER

Let me introduce you to someone whom we'll call the Teacher for now.

The Teacher remembers saying with heartfelt inspiration when she was young, "I'm going to be a teacher. I can feel it…this is me!" Recently, she reflected, "I just loved to learn and then share what I had learned. You know, teaching others springs from my talents and personality."

While in college (and as part of her careful plan), she took education courses and was a substitute teacher at a nearby school. After graduation, however, her life took a turn. She married her sweetheart, brought three children into this world, and stepped away from the classroom.

"I didn't continue as a classroom teacher for kids. I stepped out of the teachers' lobby at school and into taking care of a family at home," she shared.

Now in her eighties, the Teacher noted, "In my life as a homemaker, I changed roughly 4,500 diapers, plus or minus a thousand. I cleaned 10,000 toilets, plus or minus a few. I made about 6,000 school lunches. I spent untold hours ironing, wiping counters, picking up, making meals, doing dishes, washing clothes, paying bills, and taking care of pets." Many times, she wondered if she had what it took to be a mom: "Of all the hard jobs around, one of the hardest is being a mom!"

Though she didn't spend her adult life teaching in a classroom, she taught every single day. "I loved teaching my children about anything in the world around them. I poured myself into being a mom." Teaching her kids to "look both ways" and counting "one, two, two and a half" seems like yesterday to her. She recounts the pouts, smiles, bandages, hectic schedules, and less-than-stellar music recitals. She also recalls the joy.

Taking a closer look at the Teacher, we see a continued pattern of learning and instruction. She whispered, "I've been a Sunday school teacher, child evangelism leader, Bible Study Fellowship leader, women's fellowship leader, coffee break leader, and Crossroads Prison Ministry teacher. I had many other roles I just can't recall. And it's not important that I do."

Recently, the Teacher and the love of her life celebrated their sixtieth wedding anniversary with their children, grandchildren, and great-grandchildren. I was there with my wife of more than 30 years and our three children. Why was I there? Ah, the Teacher is my mom.

During the weeklong anniversary celebration, can you guess who shared a fun poem she'd memorized 70 years earlier? Can you guess who clarified right and wrong, inspired hope, ignited imaginations, and instilled a love of learning during our week together? Can you suppose who reminded us that God's generosity is abundant, that the Lord's mercy is incomparable, and that His love for all is beyond any measure? You guessed it.

Many years ago, my mother couldn't have imagined how her life would unfold. All along, though, God had an amazing plan for her. And in His rule, He continues to use and bless her. Even today, questions of *Why, Mom?* echo in her ears as her wisdom-filled responses resonate in our own.

Lord, thank You for loving and using my mom. Love remains.

—————— FURTHER REFLECTION AND APPLICATION ——————

Many years ago, English journalist Arthur Dunkerley, who also wrote under the name John Oxenham, wrote his poem "Gratitude for Work." The poem begins: "Upon thy bended knees, thank God for work—Work—once man's penance, now his high reward! For work to do, and strength to do the work, we thank thee, Lord!"

In this poem and in other writings, Arthur expressed gratitude for life and work. In this spirit, consider a single thing, whatever it is, for which you are most thankful at work. Hold it in your thoughts for a while. Consider where it ultimately came from, and then be sure to thank your Father in heaven.

In the New Testament, we see Paul's greetings to the people who've supported him in his work. In Romans 16:13, for example, we read of Paul's specific gratitude: "Greet Rufus, chosen in the Lord, and his mother, who has been a mother to me, too." Although the Bible doesn't mention Paul's parents, in this verse we see heart-felt acknowledgment of his friend's caring mother.

Today, with Arthur and Paul's leading, take time to share your gratitude with others for their labor. For example, send a note of appreciation to a former teacher. Reach out to edify a person who coached or invested in you along the way. Are you willing to do this? Or simply express your thankfulness to someone performing an unrewarding task nearby. My strong hunch is that they'll be appreciative and most surprised!

This is a short poem I wrote:

> My father kneels at the side of my bed, closes his eyes, pauses, and lowers his head. For many years, I've known that he cares for me, because at the end of another day, again, he offers up our prayers.[6]

I offer the following prayer you can pray now as you continue your journey of work.

> *Merciful Father, thank You for the blessing of labor by which I can worship You, serve others, and provide for needs. When I look ahead, You say, "My thoughts are not your thoughts, neither are your ways My ways" and "As the heavens are higher than the earth, so are My ways higher than your ways and My thoughts than your thoughts."*
>
> *I know You've called me to work, and You're already there with me even in what may seem like mundane labor. In my obedient response to Your invitation to work, help me to apply the qualities of King David's heart—taking steps forward, embracing change, and being wholehearted. Immanuel, as Your workmanship, please work in me and through my hands each day—write my work story—as a part of Your redeeming plan. I'm Your undimmed work in progress, and I exist every hour to display Your glory. Teach my song to rise to You in work worth doing. Guide me in the way everlasting. Amen.*

May the favor of the Lord our God rest on us;
establish the work of our hands for us—
yes, establish the work of our hands.

Psalm 90:17

ADDITIONAL MATERIAL

WHAT'S MOST IMPORTANT TO YOU?

What have I been blessed to learn? What do I know that's of most value? Well, on a lighter note, never order spaghetti for lunch. And never try to iron a shirt while wearing it.

On a more serious note, however, I'd like to share something I learned at a corporate meeting. It's about knowing what's most important.

The expansive room was filled with seated leaders from our global company. I don't recall what preceded my move from enjoying a seat to participating in a team-building exercise, but there I was, standing in front of the gathering, oddly nervous with arms crossed tightly as I listened to polished instructions from a facilitator.

"All right, please turn your back to this table, on which are several objects under this sheet. Don't turn around until I tell you, okay?" Then he said, "Keeping this simple, your goal is to get the most points. You may pick up only one object at a time with one hand, and then you must place it in your other hand. No scooping or grabbing more than one object at a time, or you'll have to start over."

And then without much of a pause, the facilitator yelled, "Go!" I spun around. The sheet was gone, and strewn across the table were poker chips, mostly white. Poker chips? But then, after no more than ten seconds of participation, he hollered, "Stop!"

My heart continued to race, but thankfully, my hands had been quick.

The facilitator grinned, took the chips from my hand, and then tallied my score. "How many white chips did he get?" he asked the group. With counting assistance from the facilitator, "Seven," replied the leaders. How many red chips? "Zero," replied the team. Green? "Zero."

Continuing, the facilitator told us the white chips were worth a single point each, red chips were worth 100 points each, and the green chips were worth 1,000 points each. My score was a whopping seven points.

Not exactly my best effort.

With a focus on speed and no knowledge of a point system, I had ignored the red and green chips on the far side of the table. And with my low score and undeclared excuses, I meandered back to my seat.

The takeaways were obvious. During the debrief, I heard the collective insights: "Don't get lost in the urgent." "Be sure to clarify the goal before getting busy." "At work and in life, focus on what's most important."

At first, the exercise felt like an embarrassment. However, the experience left a lasting impression, practical for both work and home. After all, what was vitally important to me? Was I focused on the right things?

Having clear priorities is a good thing! Certainly, we spend too much time on urgent matters. And doing more things faster is no substitute for doing the right things. But the insights from this corporate exercise fell short, and it wasn't until a few years later that I understood why.

My understanding was clarified in the back of a Pizza Hut restaurant. I was there to design an applicant-selection system for all future Pizza Hut team members and restaurant managers. Surrounded by equipment, metal pans, and the smell of baking pizza, I listened to a shift supervisor discuss her operational role. That's when a simple metaphor and a pivotal truth were made known.

"Let's start with the basics," she shared. "Making a pizza starts with the right pan. Obviously, the kitchen pan will fully shape and mold the dough."

And now, an "aha" may be obvious to you as well.

Let me ask you this: "What's important to you?" Without rushing, consider your priorities and time spent, and then divide 100 points across the following areas:

LIST A

_____ family

_____ friends

_____ fitness or health

_____ work and career

_____ God

_____ leisure

_____ community

_____ money and "things"

_____ reading or study

_____ other

What areas are most important to you?

What areas have the most points?

"I GAVE THE MOST POINTS TO MY FAMILY AND TO GOD."

Here's the challenge: Every thread of creation—including each area on List A above—has the potential to compete with our Creator. But God isn't a quiet counterpoint to your hurried life! Not at all. And He doesn't seek an allotment of points or a bigger, better slice of your time.

What's vitally important is knowing what's *most* important. And the One who matters most should never be at the mercy of other important matters.

In other words, enjoy every thread of God's creation!

However, don't replace the eternal Lord with His temporary blessings. As we've established earlier, everything belongs to God. Our world belongs to God. Your work belongs to God, and God is in your work. Your soul, mind, body, talent, and passion come from your Creator. Your family, friends, health, leisure, community, possessions, technology, money, awards, studies, and "things" belong to the Lord. You bring absolutely nothing to the King of kings. And as you go, you simply return what always belonged to the One enthroned in heaven.

So what are you and I supposed to do? In faith and obedience, yield all of our many work and life priorities to God alone as the work of His hands. Let them go! And the Potter (Isaiah 64:8) will fully shape and mold every vying interest. As we sing in the old hymn, "Have Thine own way, Lord, have Thine own way; Thou art the Potter, I am the clay. Mold me and make me after Thy will, while I am waiting, yielded and still."

Again, what's important to you? Let's do this again. As you consider your priorities and how you spend your time, divide 100 points across the competing interests that God's Spirit will fully shape, inform, and guide.

LIST B

_____ family

_____ friends

_____ fitness or health

_____ work and career

_____ leisure

_____ community

_____ money and "things"

_____ reading or study

_____ other

Here's the crucial lesson: Seek first His kingdom and His righteousness (Matthew 6:33) as portrayed with the updated List B? Or seek also as seen with List A? Do you see the often-missed yet vast difference? It's a choice of one word. Author and historian John Dickson said it this way:

> The imperial descriptions of Jesus remind us that he is Lord over all things, religious and secular, spiritual and physical, private and public. He has claims, as the New Testament insists, over my finances, my career, my politics, my sex life, my intellect, my leisure, my ambitions, and my family. In short, confessing Christ as emperor is about giving

him free rein to one's life, knowing that all empires will pass into oblivion, while Christ's kingdom reigns eternal.[1]

There it is—guidance gleaned from a charred-and-dinged kitchen pan. Sure, learning from this far-from-perfect object seems odd, but God's truth will be revealed anywhere and anyhow. And as we've seen, it's often the misfit, broken, and unlikely people or things that God chooses and uses, right? So who sets your agenda? And what is your ultimate priority? Are you seeking first, seeking also, or searching not at all?

As I said up front, this book is about your work only in the context of something far more important: your life and eternity. No matter your place in life, know that you're there for a reason. Certainly, God can use anyone, and He wants to use you. In Jesus's name, may this workplace learning be a lasting blessing to you.

WHAT DO YOU BELIEVE ABOUT YOUR WORK?

Here's the scoring for this assessment: Rate each item below on a scale of 1 to 10. A rating of 1 indicates agreement with the idea on the left side; a rating of 10 indicates agreement with the idea on the right. A rating of 5 suggests you're aligned equally with both ideas. Please add all of your ratings to determine your Total Score. The lowest possible Total Score is 10 (i.e., you rated each item a 1). The highest possible score is 100 (i.e., you rated each item a 10).

1. ____	I have everything to prove.	I have nothing to prove.
2. ____	Security? Show me the money!	My security is in Christ alone.
3. ____	Work is just a way to make a living.	My job is a sacred responsibility.
4. ____	Really, work is just work.	Really, work is a blessing.
5. ____	"You must believe in yourself."	Trust God with all outcomes.
6. ____	I'm proud of what I've done.	The whole point of work is to point wholly to God.
7. ____	"Just follow your heart" (see Jeremiah 17:9).	I have a vocational calling from God.

8. ____	"Leave your faith at the door."	The workplace is an opportunity to share the good news.
9. ____	I've never gone to work with the expectation of meeting God there.	There is no place where God is not.
10. ____	I'm doing things my way.	I'm uniquely equipped for the good works God has prepared for me alone to do.
		Total Score ____

Interpretation: If you scored between 10 and 100, know that God cares about you and your work!

"But what about my total score?"

No matter your total score—from low to high—God can use anyone, and He wants to use you. Remember, the workplace has been waiting for you for a very long time!

"WHAT IF I HATE WHAT I'M DOING?"

I hate housework! You make the beds,
you do the dishes, and six months later
you have to start all over again.

—JOAN RIVERS

Your question, "What if hate what I'm doing?" is rather common. This mind-set is shared by many people. In recent decades, survey results from Gallup indicate that only one in three workers feel "involved in, enthusiastic about and committed to their work and workplace."[1] And if you hate (or are apathetic about or dissatisfied in) a job, then you're part of the exasperated majority. Let's change that! I've been there.

But be careful. A nasty work experience can unfavorably make an impact on your faith, family, health, and general outlook. Should you resign, then? Maybe. Storm out today? Probably not. But without more details, I wouldn't try to convince you otherwise.

Let's begin to figure this out. Hating what you do isn't God-glorifying and is at odds with your ultimate purpose at work. Here are five encouragements to consider.

1. TAKE YOUR CAREER OFF ITS PEDESTAL.

> *If you think of this world as a place intended simply for our*
> *happiness, you find it quite intolerable: think of it as a place*
> *of training and correction and it's not so bad.*[2]
>
> —C.S. Lewis

Unrealistic expectations about jobs inflame workers' resentments across our tumbled world. Unfortunately, with overly high hopes, countless laborers give their all to work. Consumed, they commit to something that fails to return their commitment. In time, as they seek happiness and outcomes, the workplace disappoints them. Systems and people betray them. And then, let down and fed up, they express disgust for their work.

"What's your advice for me?"

Well, do you loathe Mondays too?

"As some say, the first five days after the weekend are the worst. Yeah, I've come to know that one of life's great joys is waking up and realizing that it's Saturday."

If that's true, lean into culture's headwinds and lower your expectations for work.

You see, work isn't the answer. A job is loved? A job was never meant to be held up, turned to, or revered. A job is hated? Any role is erratic as a source of gut-level satisfaction. And when you eye eternity, every position falls flat as a source of essential fulfillment.

If work is what you endure between weekends, let me ask this: In pride, are you preoccupied with your occupation and what comes from it? Devoted, are you neglecting personal relationships for your work? Or feeling empty and depressed, are you questioning the purpose of it all?

Remember this: No matter the blessing, your employment is passing. Despite the goodness, your networks, assignments, and close-knit teams fade away. Truly, this colorful book of work is intense but brief. So be wise! Step right up and take it down. Don't let the fleeting rewards and vocational pursuits become an ill-advised obsession.

2. PUT A SPOTLIGHT ON THE ISSUE.

The man who complains about the way the ball
bounced is likely to be the one who dropped it.

—LOU HOLTZ

A job candidate came to an on-site interview and asked the hiring manager, "Will I like working here?"

In reply, the hiring manager asked, "Did you like where you came from?"

"No," the candidate replied.

"Then it's unlikely you'll like it here."

If you despise what you're doing, put a spotlight on the issue. Is it perhaps you?

Did you hate your last job as well? And have you ever enjoyed this type of work? Be honest and then do something about it. For starters, see the seven smart-with-heart actions in chapter 5, realizing that your attitude is a choice and that insights begin with a clear understanding of yourself, the world of work, and how they come together. Or is it something in your workplace? Maybe the tasks are okay, but your supervisor or pay has you troubled.

Perhaps you just don't like your coworkers, the bottomless in-box slog, or something else about your employer or location. If your setting is uninspired, take steps ahead in faith. Push yourself to find solutions. And rather than dwelling on negatives, walk by the Spirit and ask for help with your "hate" as well as with the cunning source of this sentiment.

Still looking for more? For scriptural insights on challenging work experiences, take a moment to read the words of Ephesians 6, Colossians 3, and 1 Peter 2.

3. DO YOUR BEST.

Most people work just hard enough not to get fired
and get paid just enough money not to quit.

—GEORGE CARLIN

The apostle Paul wrote, as told in this paraphrase, "Servants, do what you're told by your earthly masters. And don't just do the minimum that will get you by. Do your best. Work from the heart for your real Master, for God, confident that you'll get paid in full when you come into your inheritance. Keep in mind always that the ultimate Master you're serving is Christ. The sullen servant who does shoddy work will be held responsible. Being a follower of Jesus doesn't cover up bad work" (Colossians 3:22-25 MSG).

Do you agree?

Are you still leaning into culture's headwinds? If so, adjust your balance and lean in even more. Because if you hate what you're doing, the world will push you to find something new. As if there's little to consider, many people will say, "Get out of there!" "It's time to make a change!" "Find a job you can enjoy!" And, why not? After all, according to them, the goal is "livin' the dream," with the fewest delays in pursuit of it.

"But unappreciated, overworked, and underpaid is no way to go through life. My job is something I care for deeply, **not** *about."*

I know it's not easy. But I sense that you do care about it.

Well, what's more challenging than making it through another day in a place like this?"

Here's something more challenging: No matter your feelings, do your best! As stated in Colossians 3:23-25, your work standard is to glorify God no matter how you feel about it. Beyond a blue-sky notion, respond in faith with your highest-quality work. At a minimum, strive to be the most honest, respectful, and dignified person there. Strive toward what's ahead. Surrounded by incompetence? Challenge the status quo rather than work within it. Spinning your wheels? Reassess any goals that seek only modest change or marginal improvement.

"Whew! And be sure to get to work early, never take too many sick days, and have alphabetized content in my pantry at home? I'm exhausted just thinking about it."

I get it. Faced with the choice of accepting Colossians 3:23-35 or looking for another opportunity, most get busy with their job search. But know this: The Lord will use anything—even a position or place you can't stand—to prepare you for what's next. The relationships you make, the wisdom you gain, and situations you experience are all a part of His incredible plan.

4. FIND HUMBLE TASKS.

I long to accomplish a great and noble task, but it is my chief duty to accomplish humble tasks as though they were great and noble. The world is moved along, not only by the mighty shoves of its heroes, but also by the aggregate of the tiny pushes of each honest worker.[3]

—HELEN KELLER

If you don't like what you're doing, here's a fourth encouragement: Seek the tiny pushes; find the humble tasks. As the Great "I AM," Jesus Christ did so. To serve, the Name above all names washed the disciples' dirty feet with water from a basin (John 13:5). And in these small motivations we see a key part of our definition of work: "to uplift others." This is how workers find their lost smiles. This is where labor as a *sacred responsibility* makes most sense.

Here's how tiny pushes make change. The wholehearted action of a humble worker is an amazing antidote to the prideful want of more: the desire to gain more power. To achieve more. To grab attention and more time. And as a rich source of madness, just more of "whatever" than someone else has.

"So should we take off our shoes?"

What?

"I'll find a bucket and get some soapy water."

Oh, I'm sorry. That's not what I intended. Rather, act as a humble worker in whatever job you're in! At your worksite, with prayer, take a different path amid those challenging responsibilities. Losing your hate occurs when you seek to provide help. To offer attention and more time. And as a rich source of joy, just more of "whatever" for someone else.

In our rush, too often we underestimate the impact of unexpected help, a kind word, a sincere compliment, or the smallest act of caring. So, then, in your expected busyness, seek to give "whatever" for others. With renewed purpose, make marginal adjustments to your daily routine. However, recognize that your tiny pushes may not alter the worksite. Regrettably, your thoughtful touches may go unnoticed, and your small deeds may not leave a mark. But if you hate your job, guess what? There's an honest chance that the aggregate of your quiet contributions will begin to change you.

5. BE WILLING TO LEAVE YOUR JOB.

Are you sure you want to quit?
All unsaved progress will be lost.
—Nintendo

Be willing to leave your job? The disciples did. Without delay, Peter and Andrew walked off the job without giving two weeks' notice: "At once they left their nets and followed him" (Matthew 4:20). Also, in the Old Testament, Joseph and Nehemiah willingly moved from servant roles to government leaders. And among many positions, David shifted between poet, shepherd, warrior, and king.

Here are two questions to consider if you're pondering a job change: Is your motivation glorifying to God? And have you made the most of this opportunity? (See Colossians 4:2-6 and Titus 2:10.)

Those are tough questions, but your challenge is to commit to God whatever you do and be fully available to Him as you go. Now, if you decide to leave your job at some point, so be it. Take good care. As you follow Him, it's not an affront to the King of kings if you change positions or employer loyalties. Why would it be? And no matter how long you stay (potential spoiler alert), there's no eternal plaque for high tenure. Our Lord isn't as concerned with a job hop as He is with *why* you work each day.

In a mood-poisoning situation, you may feel as if each day provides justification for a hasty decision, but you can and should take your time! Be thoughtful and deliberate. That said, many workers stay too long in these settings for various reasons. Feeling trapped, they remain where fear, power, and intimidation coexist in comfort. But why? If where you are is mentally or physically abusive, get out.

And if it's immoral, destructive, unethical, or a barrier to intimacy with God, find another role right away.

Begin praying that your heavenly Father will confirm your decision to quit your job. As His handiwork, God may very well open a new opportunity for you. As a co-laborer in any job, God is at work in and through you to do the work He intends. Or, to your surprise, your Creator may change your current work experience. Or the Holy Spirit may help you to understand your circumstance in a new or different way.

Starting here, I hope these encouragements are helpful to you in some way. And remember, when work puts a bitter taste on your tongue, even when you don't understand why, trust the Lord of the workplace with all outcomes.

HOW TO FIND A GREAT JOB

"What's the smart-with-heart way to land a great job?"

I appreciate this question! Within the field of Human Resources, the topic of job search has been an interest of mine for years. This passion led me to help design applicant selection systems for some of the world's most-recognized companies.

Here are ten tips to help you land a great job. Some of them will be a review of what we've already covered.

1. *Be open.* As a believer, the initial step to land a great job is to listen. Above all else, recall that a calling is the work to which God calls you. He initiates this direct demand and communication. Then let Him continue to mold and guide you and your search. Why? A calling response goes beyond listening to being open and available before God.

2. *Avoid barbers.* Again, listen to a varied group of God's people. Seek your pastor, teachers, or career counselors who can provide encouragement and insights about your uniqueness. Ask knowledge holders and position holders to share their wisdom with you. But never ask a barber or stylist if you need a haircut. And likewise, don't seek career advice from those who have something to gain from your decision.

3. *Know yourself.* Step away from your résumé, online profile, and phone. Take a big step into self-reflection. Most of the time, increased self-awareness will outdo the résumé keyword tricks and networking breakfasts. From our smart-with-heart

actions (chapter 5), be clear about your gold stars and passions. Understand your patterns of pain. And be honest about your motivations, who you really are, and what you're really not.

4. *Think ahead.* Like an architect, start with the end in mind. One way is to consider the labor market. For a data-driven approach, as an example, be familiar with the Bureau of Labor Statistics (BLS) or your country's equivalent. Can you project out a few years? Please don't be like the recent graduate in oceanography who was surprised by the limited opportunities in Nebraska or Alberta.

5. *Get connected.* The majority of job openings aren't posted. They're found only in the so-called "hidden" job market. So how do you uncover these opportunities? In addition to your own connections, one of the best ways is through a professional recruiter. If you want to land a great job, get to know the leading recruiter in the targeted area or field. Who is this? Is your information in his or her hands? And have you made yourself an obvious choice?

6. *Be prepared.* Having interviewed job candidates for a few decades, believe me when I say that many aren't prepared for the moment. Remember, you're competing with others! Show up with extra copies of your résumé/curriculum vitae. Always do research on the organization. Push yourself to review any available financial statements. And practice your explanation of any short stints or gaps in employment.

7. *Sell yourself.* If you're not clear on why someone should hire you, they won't be clear about that either. What makes you the obvious choice? Be willing to share your accomplishments! Communicate your actions and specific results. The interview team isn't looking for a nice new friend. They want you to explain how you'll contribute to their organization.

8. *Know the boss.* Don't take a job without knowing the supervisor. This person must be a visible part of the selection process. Try to identify what makes them tick; seek out their values and priorities. Did you get an employment offer? Trust me. If you don't know the supervisor or he or she just isn't a clear fit, save yourself some serious heartache and walk away up front.

9. *Jump into the pool.* From our smart-with-heart actions, clarity in becoming what God intended you to be is most often a natural by-product of time and

doing. With swimming, as well as our work, clarity about what to do often comes with just getting in there. And even when an *It's not exactly what I'm looking for* job comes along, express your interest anyway.

10. *Be thankful.* Yes, your work will be the most bewildering, truly remarkable, and time-consuming blessing you'll ever receive. And when you receive your job, be sure to thank God for the blessing it is, no matter what it is. After all, it's a gift. Long ago, the Lord chose it for you!

So, then, what's the best way to land a great job? Consider *My work opportunity is nowhere.*

A typical answer is to make sense of this apparent misprint by interpreting it as *My work opportunity IS NOWHERE.*

But this answer isn't in line with our ten tips for landing a great job, right?

Look at it again. A few seconds spent coming up with an alternative will yield *My work opportunity is now here.* And it really is! As part of your calling response, God wants to use you to help accomplish His purposes right now.

I hope these ten ideas are helpful in some way. But if you become deflated by this endeavor, remember that the Bible says God has a plan for you. You've been preciously chosen, divinely anointed, strategically placed, and fully empowered to work with God right now.

KEY POINTS AND SCRIPTURE REFERENCES

CHAPTER 1: GOD CAN USE ANYONE

KEY POINTS

- God can use anyone, and He wants to use you.
- God will use anyone to accomplish His purposes.
- Work is useful. It glorifies God and uplifts others.
- Your work is a divine blessing and responsibility.

SCRIPTURE REFERENCES

A short while back, I walked into a church with my mother-in-law. As I was opening the front door for her, she exclaimed, "Oh, no. I've forgotten my Bible!" She then paused for a moment, took just enough time to think about the pastor, and said, without trying to be funny, "I guess I'll just have to trust him." Her comment certainly made me smile. In this book, the cited Bible verses are listed here for your reference.

Genesis 3
Numbers 22:28
1 Samuel 16:1,6-7,12, 14-23;
    17:28,45
2 Samuel 7:8-16,29

Job 9:8,10
Psalm 147:4
Acts 13:22
Matthew 22:37-39
Ephesians 2:10; 3:20

CHAPTER 2: WORK IS *WORK*

Key Points

- Work is infused with pain and strain.
- Jesus worked for years in a common role not held in high regard.
- Jesus was tested in all respects, just like you.
- Jesus wants to use you where you are.

Scripture References

Genesis 1:28; 3
Isaiah 9:6
Matthew 5:16; 7:24-27; 9:9; 21:28-31
Mark 6:3 NLT and MSG
Luke 15:11-16
John 1:14; 10:1-11
Ephesians 2:2
Hebrews 4:15 MSG

CHAPTER 3: WHAT'S THE POINT?

KEY POINTS

- God alone is the source and ultimate goal of our work.
- You work to glorify Him.
- All of your work is worthwhile.
- God is in your workplace.

SCRIPTURE REFERENCES

Genesis 22:14; 28:16-17
Deuteronomy 10:14
Psalms 24:1 NASB; 93:1; 139:8
Isaiah 43:7
John 6:35
Romans 11:36
1 Corinthians 10:26,31; 12:7
Ephesians 2:10; 6:7
Colossians 3:23 NLT
1 Thessalonians 5:18
1 Peter 4:10

CHAPTER 4: YOUR WHY

KEY POINTS

- You are amazing. No, really!
- God selected your path.
- Any separation of work and worship is wrong.
- Your response to God's calling is the work you'll do today.

SCRIPTURE REFERENCES

Genesis 3:17; 22
Psalm 40:7; 139:13-14
Isaiah 6:8; 49:16
Daniel 5:5
Matthew 2:7-8; 25:15
Romans 12:4-5
1 Corinthians 12:7,12,20,27
Galatians 3:26
Ephesians 2:10
Hebrews 10:7-9
2 Timothy 1:6 NASB; 3:17
1 Peter 4:11 NASB
Revelation 12:11

CHAPTER 5: SMART-WITH-HEART ACTIONS

KEY POINTS

- Know you can't please everyone.
- Connect your gold stars.
- Explore your patterns of pain.
- Jump into the pool.
- Seize the smaller opportunities around you.
- Trust God with all outcomes.
- Declare dependence.

SCRIPTURE REFERENCES

Genesis 39:23
Psalms 25:14; 139:23-24
Proverbs 3:5-6; 11:14 ESV; 16:3; 20:24 ESV
Matthew 3:17 ESV
John 16:33
Romans 8:26
Galatians 1:10
1 Timothy 6:10
James 1:5; 4:13-16
1 Peter 4:10 NLT

CHAPTER 6: TAKING STEPS FORWARD

KEY POINTS

- God has been looking at hearts since He created the first one.
- Three qualities of David's heart apply to you and your work:
  - » taking steps forward (chapter 6)
  - » embracing change (chapter 7)
  - » being wholehearted (chapter 8)
- God encourages us many times with the words *Do not be afraid.*
- Do and say what's not easy to do and say—each day.

SCRIPTURE REFERENCES

Deuteronomy 3:22; 31:6 ESV
Joshua 1:3 NASB
Joshua 1:9 ESV
1 Samuel 14:44; 15:10-31; 16:14; 17; 18:6-8,12; 20:30-34
1 Chronicles 18
Psalms 3:1-6; 23:4; 27:1; 111:10; 118:7; 121:1-2
Proverbs 1:7; 19:23
Ecclesiastes 2:11
Isaiah 41:10
Matthew 25:35-36
Acts 13:22
2 Timothy 1:7 ESV
1 John 4:17-18

CHAPTER 7: EMBRACING CHANGE

KEY POINTS

- You are surrounded by disruptive change in the workplace.
- All change is divinely guided.
- The only thing constant in change is God.
- Embrace change and abide in what's constant.

SCRIPTURE REFERENCES

Genesis 39:23
Exodus 35:30-35
1 Samuel 18:14
Psalms 18:2; 57:7 NLT; 62:6; 89:11; 90:1-2 MSG
Proverbs 6:6 KJV
Isaiah 46:4
Malachi 3:6 KJV
1 Corinthians 7:7
2 Thessalonians 1:11
Hebrews 13:8 MSG

CHAPTER 8: BEING WHOLEHEARTED

KEY POINTS

- Your work enables you to be close to God.
- Beware of the desire for more, pride in self, and being halfhearted. They are barriers to intimacy with God.
- Because of God's grace, you have nothing to prove.
- God's invitation to intimacy applies to your labor today and to your active service forevermore.

SCRIPTURE REFERENCES

Psalms 9:1-2; 18:1; 23:1; 34:1; 36:7; 51; 63:1; 90:17
Ecclesiastes 1:11
Isaiah 55:8-9; 64:6
Jeremiah 29:13
Matthew 25:14-30
Luke 12:13-21; 19:10
John 6:28-29; 14:6
Romans 10:9-10; 16:13
1 Corinthians 2:9 KJV; 15:58 NLT
2 Corinthians 4:17-18 MSG
Ephesians 2:8-10
Revelation 7:15; 21:1,3-5; 22:3

GOING DEEPER

CHAPTER 1: GOD CAN USE ANYONE

A. This highlight review of David's life is based on a sermon series from teaching pastor Kyle Idleman, serving at Southeast Christian Church in Louisville, Kentucky. Kyle's series looked at people of faith and their place in the surprising twists and turns in God's perfect plan. Although I wasn't singled out by the pastor, God spoke to me clearly the day Kyle spoke about David.

- David is anointed king in 1 Samuel 16:13. (Interestingly, in the thirteenth century it took the College of Cardinals almost three years to anoint a successor to Pope Clement IV. To break this deadlock, one of history's most bitter organizational stalemates, church officials limited the food and drink they provided to the voting cardinals. Eventually, they provided the voters with just bread and water. Fortunately for all involved, the anointing of young David as the successor to King Saul took less than a day.)

- David kills Goliath after downing him with a single stone from his sling (1 Samuel 17:49).

- David becomes a commander in the army and then spends years hiding from Saul after David and Saul have a falling out (1 Samuel 18 through 1 Samuel 26).

- David is finally made king over all Israel (2 Samuel 5).

B. Here are Scripture passages to read the stories about:

- Mary, who became Jesus's mother (Luke 1:26-38)
- Jonah (the book of Jonah)
- Joshua (the book of Joshua)
- Matthew (Matthew 9:9)
- Joseph (beginning in Genesis 37)

CHAPTER 2: WORK IS *WORK*

A. I visited three internet sites to find the worst, most dangerous, and lowest paying jobs. Here is where I found carpenter on each list:

- **Worst:** #147. Accessed June 15, 2019, http://www.independent.co.uk/news/uk/home-news/revealed-news-reporter-is-the-worst-job-in-the-world-but-its-good-news-for-death-for-death-predictors-8586327.html

- **Most dangerous:** #23. Accessed June 15, 2019, http://list25.com/25-most-dangerous-jobs-in-the-world/

- **Lowest paying:** #204. Accessed June 15, 2019, http://www.myplan.com/careers/top-ten/lowest-paying.php

B. Saint Francis of Assisi said, "The deeds you do may be the only sermon some persons will hear today." As you faithfully work with cynics or skeptics, for inspiration, read 1 Timothy 6:1; recall that Daniel served loyally in Nebuchadnezzar's court (Daniel 2); and note that Joseph worked with the Egyptians to alleviate famine (Genesis 41). Related, and emphasizing the connection between God's work and our work, Pope John Paul II stated, "By our labor we are unfolding the Creator's work and contributing to the realization of God's plan on earth." And more recently, Pope Francis noted, "Every Christian can witness to God in the workplace, not only with words, but above all with an honest life."

CHAPTER 3: WHAT'S THE POINT?

A. Does God care about what happens in a supermarket or retail outlet store? Is the Creator of the universe dwelling in an aisle at Walmart? According to Scripture, He really does, and He really is. Whether you're surrounded by money, beside contented strangers, or in underserved localities, God is there. Yep, it doesn't matter if your working time just flies by or feels longer than any eight hours has a right to. The Holy Spirit is still with you.

In *Where Is God at Work?* tax lawyer and priest William Morris shared the following:

> If God can meet Jacob in the middle of nowhere, put down a ladder from heaven and transform his life, then I think I owe it to God to exercise my imagination and keep my eyes open in unlikely places, including at Tesco (a large retailer). So, I always tell them a story. My wife has an uncle who lives in a rural part of the northern US. In the sixties, he was countercultural and never wanted to work in an office or a factory, so he lived on the family farm. When kids came along, he realized he needed health insurance, so he went to the local supermarket and signed on to stack shelves for the hours necessary to get coverage. He's now been doing this for decades. He does it well. It has supported his family. The customers in the store know him, and he brings a smile to their faces. Many people might think that he hankers to be a two talent or a five-talent slave (servant), but actually he doesn't. And who are we to say that being part of a chain of commerce that brings food at reasonable prices to people who perhaps don't have much cash—and also bringing a smile to their face at the same time—is not helping to build God's kingdom?[1]

B. Jeff Van Duzer, in *Why Business Matters to God*, states the following:

> Analyzing a spreadsheet, preparing a quarterly income statement and entering into a lease agreement are acts that from the standpoint of the outside observer may look the same regardless of the faith of the practitioner. But from the inside it makes all the difference. If Christians can understand that the work they are doing is God's work they can

bring a sense of joy, meaning, purpose, pride and hope to their tasks that might otherwise elude them.[2]

Concurring, Ben Witherington III wrote the following in *Work: A Kingdom Perspective on Labor*:

> The truth is that even when work seems like drudgery, if it is done to God's glory it is good in character, and if it is done for the edification of others it is at the very least divine drudgery, not mere toil, not mere activity. It has meaning, purpose, direction. It is Kingdom-bringing.[3]

C. You're wondering if all jobs are equal. Let's look at what A. W. Tozer wrote in a book titled *The Pursuit of God*:

> Paul's exhortation to do everything for the glory of God is more than pious idealism. It is an integral part of the sacred revelation and is to be accepted as the very Word of Truth. It opens before us the possibility of making every act of our lives contribute to the glory of God.[4]

Tozer continued by saying the following.

> It does not mean, for instance, that everything we do is of equal importance with everything else we do or may do…Paul's sewing of tents was not equal to his writing of an Epistle to the Romans, but both were accepted of God and both were true acts of worship. Certainly, it is more important to lead a soul to Christ than to plant a garden, but the planting of the garden can be as holy an act as the winning of a soul.[5]

Tozer distinguished between actions based on enduring kingdom impact but emphasized that all work is accepted of God.

"Got it."

Taking this concept further, let's tease apart three often-entangled terms— market value, meaningfulness, and intrinsic worth.

People make distinctions between jobs based on the market value of labor—that is, what a specific job pays. In a Human Resources department, a compensation professional formally orders a company's jobs relative to market value to set pay rates. And in your marketplace, for take-home pay, a few make a lot and a lot likely make a little.

"Sure, jobs aren't all paid the same wage."

Next, consider with me the personal meaningfulness of work. Former US President Teddy Roosevelt supposed, "Far and away the best prize that life offers is the chance to work hard at work worth doing." And like this president—and inspired by the words of Ecclesiastes 2:24—"A person can do nothing better than to eat and drink and find satisfaction in their own toil"—and inspired "to do good" by Ecclesiastes 3:12, you may see some work as having more meaning or being of greater service to others. After some discernment, you may seek meaningfulness in the form of a unique challenge or where tasks are key to social impact and personal reward.

"Some jobs have more meaning than others."

For me too. And now, let's consider the intrinsic worth of labor. As Jesus hammered home, from God's perspective, all work—from the paid to pro bono—is worthy. God created your work and gives it meaning. Either He defines its worth or it has none. Best considered, your work isn't a means to an end but rather worthiness in and of itself. Thus, you can bring glory to Him and serve others in whatever role you're in! No job is better than any other job—there's no difference in the worth or value of any labor.

In *A Parable of the Wicked Mammon*, William Tyndale, who translated the Bible into English, wrote, "There is no work better than another to please God: to pour water, to wash dishes, to be a souter (cobbler), or an apostle, all is one; to wash dishes and to preach is all one, as touching the deed, to please God."[6]

So let's summarize: Jobs vary in opportunity for kingdom impact, market value, and meaningfulness. However, in our Creator's eyes, all jobs are worthy, and all parts of the body are needed for the body to function properly.

D. In his book *God at Work: Your Christian Vocation in All of Life*, Gene Edward Veith Jr. suggests that when you understand it properly, Martin Luther's doctrine of vocation—"doing everything for God's glory"—is not a platitude or an outdated notion.

> This principle that we vaguely apply to our lives and our work is actually the key to Christian ethics, to influencing our culture for Christ, and to infusing our ordinary, everyday lives with the presence of God. For when we realize that the "mundane" activities that consume most of our time are "God's hiding places," our perspective changes.[7]

Worth noting, relative to a "lofty work standard," he advised the following:

> There is no distinctively Christian way of being a carpenter, or an actor or a musician. Christian and non-Christian factory workers, farmers, lawyers, and bankers do pretty much the same thing. Perhaps a Christian might be unusually honest or ethical, but honesty and ethical behavior is expected of the non-Christian worker as well. Remember that non-Christians too have been placed in their positions and are being used by the God they do not even know.[8]

To be clear, as a believer, you have a distinct work purpose—you work to be obedient to God and to glorify Him. For a reminder of your vastly different and elevated standard, see the Heidelberg Catechism, Lord's Day 49: "Help us one and all to carry out the work we are called to as willingly and faithfully as the angels in heaven." How's that for a high bar!

Yes, many times, your habits and behaviors may be the same for you as for a nonbeliever. That's because diligence, determination, and high work standards aren't exclusive to believers. And though we live in a fragmented world, a decent sense of "rightness" is ingrained by God into the way all work gets done.

One more thing. Although possibly tempting, some work is work you should never do. Stating the obvious, some jobs aren't vocations and some professions aren't tied to God's calling. What does this mean for you? Know that

God's Spirit will provide guidance to you about your work. The Holy Spirit won't lead you to a job that entails sinning or that divides your heart (e.g., who has your heart—God or money? See Matthew 6:24; 1 Timothy 6:10.). And you won't be called to tasks that are immoral, destructive, harmful to others (as you are to be your "brother's keeper"), or a barrier to intimacy with God.

E. Certainly, God is revealed in Saturn's rings. As we read in Psalm 19:1-2, "The heavens proclaim the glory of God. The skies display his craftsmanship. Day after day they continue to speak; night after night they make him known" (NLT). After reading about Jesus and His craftsman's role in chapter 2, can you appreciate more the careful choice of the word *craftsmanship* in this translation of Psalm 19? And can you relate even more to the old hymn "How Great Thou Art" when singing, "O Lord my God, when I in awesome wonder / consider all the worlds Thy hands have made / I see the stars, I hear the rolling thunder / Thy power throughout the universe displayed"?

CHAPTER 4: YOUR WHY

A. How does "deliciousness of work" fit with cleaning toilets, "pump outs" of boat-contained human excrement, and other crappy tasks? Some refer to this distasteful work as "cleaning the Augean stable." Augeas, a mythical king, kept grand stables that held 3,000 oxen and had not been cleaned for three decades—until Hercules was assigned an odorous washing task. According to mythology, Hercules completed this task by causing two rivers to run through the stables. Deliciousness of work? I wouldn't call this foul-scented work "delicious." Augean tasks, Augean labor, and others like them are inspired, though, no matter how unsanitary. Most assuredly, this toil is a divine calling. All work is worth doing. At the same time, this type of work is a nasty grind and a trial for most people to complete.

B. Ben Witherington III states the following about calling:

> Calling and work go together in the Kingdom, and this is perfectly apparent from Jesus' initial calling of the Twelve. What did he say,

after all, but "Follow me, and I will make you fishers of human beings" (Mark 1:17). Following is, of course, an activity, a doing of something, and more to the point, *being "fishers of human beings" is a job description.*[9]

Later in the book he says,

> Luther's understanding of "staying in one's station in life and seeing it as one's calling and/or vocation from God" of course also flies in the face of the evidence of the Gospels, where Jesus calls disciples *away* from their nets, *away* from tax collecting, and, in Jesus' own case, away from carpentry.[10]

C. If you've ever gazed at the sky to understand your calling, you're not alone. The Reverend Billy Graham's family has passed down a story about him and his younger brother Melvin. Years ago, when Billy and Melvin were on the family's dairy farm, they saw a plane meant for advertising. In the sky, the plane drew out the letters "GP."

Billy looked at it and said, "I think that means 'Go preach.'"

His brother looked at it and said, "I think it means 'Go plow.'" So Melvin Graham ran the dairy farm, and Billy Graham spent decades advancing the gospel.

When the Reverend Graham died, his nephew, Deryl Graham, relayed this family story. And he vowed that, as far as he knows, every word of it is true.[11]

CHAPTER 5: SMART-WITH-HEART ACTIONS

A. When I was just starting out, I was confused at times too. While pursuing a degree in psychology, I was seeking to apply my newfound school learning to a business setting. Here are excerpts from a rejection letter I received from the Executive Director at the Chicago Metropolitan Center (CMC):

> Your college has forwarded your application for the CMC Semester to us. The staff has reviewed it, given it serious consideration, and decided that at this point we cannot accept you into the program. Please let me explain.

As you recall, when I and my assistant were at your school, the two of us spent 45 minutes talking with you about your educational and career goals. At that time, we strongly suggested that prior to your applying to the CMC Program, you realistically reassess your present career goals, and engage in further career counseling and exploration. That time represented career counseling from two individuals, who are "out in the field," who can realistically evaluate the kinds of internships "the marketplace" is offering and the kinds of jobs available for college graduates in their early twenties.

Further, we spoke with you about our difficulty in placing students with Psychology majors in Business. When businesses are accepting interns from liberal arts colleges, they almost unanimously insist on Business majors.

A year ago we had a young man on the program with a nearly 4.0 GPA, a Psychology major and a Business minor. He interviewed at four businesses in Chicago, two for Marketing and two for Personnel, and was turned down by all four. At that point, he had the choice to return to his college, or, as he chose, do an internship where he could more traditionally use his Psychology major. Tom, I would not want that to happen to you.

Tom, I realize that this letter may distress you. I've often thought about you since our chat and wondered how you were progressing. I ask that you take this as a positive challenge toward self-assessment. You've a keen interest in helping people that I admire; I trust that you can find some tangible channels where you can use your gifts to serve others.

Whew! This rejection letter may just as well have read, "Tom, the staff has reviewed your application, given it serious consideration, and now…into the vast wilderness you go!" And feeling the ache of things disassembled, I returned to my apartment and curled up under the bedcovers for a bit. With my solitary pity party and complaints, unwittingly, I approximately echoed the Israelites, who when in the desert with Moses cried, "Is the LORD among us or not!" (Exodus 17:7).

B. About a hundred years ago, the so-named father of vocational guidance, Frank Parsons, theorized that insights begin with a clear understanding of yourself, the world of work, and how they come together.

In the same vein, college president Gordon T. Smith wrote these insight-ful lines:

> We can consider what God is doing that might be catching our atten-tion, and we might be moved by many possibilities. But then we also need to ask…Who am I? Or, much like the urging of the Apostle Paul to the Romans, we each need to take a considered, patient and honest look at ourselves (Rom 12:3).

> Sober self-reflection is an essential counterpart to our delight in the work of God. We might easily be inspired by what others are doing for and with God. But self-knowledge is critical to the process of voca-tional discernment.

> There is no substitute for a solid, clear-minded, sober look at ourselves.

> God's call on our lives is consistent with who God made us to be.

> It is not about who we *wish* we were, but who we *actually* are.

> Self-knowledge is not, then, an act of selfishness or self-centeredness, but an act of stewardship, of seeing ourselves in truth so that we can live in truth for Christ and for others.[12]

Concurring, Ken Costa wrote, "The better we know ourselves, the more we can imagine what kind of work God might be calling us to."[13]

In addition, Lee Hardy noted:

> We were not born with job descriptions taped to our backs. Our voca-tional aptitudes have to be discovered in that process by which we come to know ourselves. But the road to self-knowledge can be a long one, and often we don't possess a clear idea of exactly what our talents are at the time we must make vocational decisions. If we are not sure what we are good at, it often pays to reflect upon our past experience with precisely that question in mind.[14]

C. The finding about "fit" was shared by economist Neil Howe. Also, in *Generations: The History of America's Future, 1584 to 2069* (New York: Morrow, 1991), William Strauss and Neil Howe articulated their idea of generations as related to employment. In *Millennials Rising: The Next Great Generation* (New York: Vintage Books, 2000), they expanded considerably on the millennial generation.

D. You said, "I want to figure this out and then get a job!" Many millennials in the workplace want "it" now, whatever "it" happens to be. In a sense, with restlessness handed down, there's a desire to fast-forward to the conclusion.

With a focus on patience, King David wrote, "Wait for the LORD; be strong and let your heart take courage; yes, wait for the LORD" (Psalm 27:14 NASB). Later, he wrote, "Commit your way to the LORD; trust in him and he will do this: He will make your righteous reward shine like the dawn, your vindication like the noonday sun. Be still before the LORD and wait patiently for him; do not fret when people succeed in their ways, when they carry out their wicked schemes" (Psalm 37:5-7).

"It's so hard to be patient!"

When you're feeling impatient, recall that Noah spent more than a century building an ark. For many years, before the dark clouds formed, he certainly looked like a fool. And at well past the age of 80, Moses wrote, "May the favor of the Lord our God rest on us; establish the work of our hands for us—yes, establish the work of our hands" (Psalm 90:17). Moses wanted to leave a legacy for the children who followed him. His influence wasn't over!

Remember Abraham and Sarah, who at a very late age became father and mother to sons who would become the forefathers of many nations. After many detours, Caleb led a battle into the hill country in Canaan when he was 85. Zechariah protested to the angel Gabriel at an advanced age. Anna was 84 when she identified Jesus as the Messiah while at the temple. And the apostle John was likely more than 90 years old when he penned the book of Revelation.

If you're feeling allergic to the waiting process, think of Vera Wang, renowned wedding dress designer, who until 39 only *wrote* about fashion. Did you know that painter Vincent van Gogh abandoned his work as an art dealer and a missionary at age 27 to concentrate on painting and drawing? And consider Gordon Bowker, who founded Starbucks at 51; Ray Kroc, who established McDonald's as we know it at 52; and Ferdinand Porsche, who founded the Porsche car company at 56.

Although it's not easy, trust the Potter who keeps molding and remolding us in His divine image. And know that a slow unfolding of a calling is…well, still a calling.

Further, tied to *jump into the pool* and refinement, author Lee Hardy shared the following:

> Some experimentation, then, may be required in the process of career choice. If several occupational options lie before me, and they all look equally valid and interesting, rather than allowing myself to be paralyzed by the lack of a deciding factor, it would be better simply to choose one and pursue it. In the course of pursuing that occupation I will inevitably learn something I couldn't have known prior to its pursuit. I may become convinced that I had in fact made the right choice. On the other hand, I might find out in no uncertain terms that I made the "wrong" choice. Not to worry. I can still benefit from that. I have learned something about myself. And I can cross one occupational option off my list.[15]

The common fear of getting it wrong as well as any search for the one-and-only "right job" reminds me of an article in *The Onion* titled "97-Year-Old Dies Unaware of Being Violin Prodigy." In this made-up story, the article begins as follows:

> Retired post office branch manager Nancy Hollander, 97, died at her home of natural causes Tuesday, after spending her life completely unaware that she was one of the most talented musicians of the past century and possessed the untapped ability to become a world-class violin virtuoso. She is survived by two daughters, a son, six grandchildren,

and three great-grandchildren, all of whom will forever remain oblivious to the national treasure Hollander would have become had she just picked up a violin even once.[16]

E. Let's cover another practical opportunity: shadowing. There's nothing mysterious about this. Tag along and be a sponge. Soak up everything while observing someone in the trenches. And inquire about required training as well as job prospects. Talk with someone who's done it before. This isn't a cutting-edge concept; job shadowing has been around since the first long beards, fiery chariots, and male-pattern baldness (2 Kings 2:23). Elisha shadowed the prophet Elijah for several years. And like Elisha, be sure to shadow someone who's actively engaged in the work and lifestyle you're considering.

F. Yes, God used circumstances to get His people to stop and listen. Moses saw a burning bush that didn't burn up. As he approached to learn more, the Lord spoke to him from the fire (Exodus 3:1-22). And the call of Samuel (1 Samuel 3:1-9, with God calling Samuel's name) and of the prophets, as well as of Paul in his dramatic conversion (Acts 9:1-9), all point to a God who calls directly.[17]

Prominent calls include the call of Abram (God told him to leave his country and go to a land God would show him), Genesis 12:1-3; the call of Deborah, Judges 4:4-10; the call of Isaiah, Isaiah 6:1-8 (the Lord said to Isaiah, "Whom shall I send? And who will go for us?"); the call of Jeremiah, Jeremiah 1:4-10; the call of Peter, Andrew, James, and John, Matthew 4:18-22; the call of Matthias to replace Judas, Acts 1:21-26; the call of the first deacons, Acts 6:1-6; and the call of Paul and Barnabas to the first missionary journey, Acts 13:2-3. At other times, rather than a stunning direct call, God used—and still uses—other people, settings, and instances to convey His call.

G. Here are the stories of the man known as Colonel Sanders and Daniel Nava, the major league baseball player I mentioned earlier. They might be considered "late bloomers."

Colonel Harland David Sanders is known as the founder of Kentucky Fried Chicken. That part of his story is no secret to most people. What isn't as well known is that by his forties, he had been in and out of numerous jobs—from fireman, farmhand, streetcar conductor, and steam engine stoker to black-smith's helper, insurance salesman, and filling-station operator. His volatile career included, among other things, repeated resignations, a courtroom brawl, a firing for insubordination, a pink slip due to plant closure, a dismissal from a service station, and walking papers for a clash with a colleague.

Roughed up and ragged, Harland bought a small service station, motel, and restaurant in his hometown of North Corbin, Kentucky. And there he began selling fried chicken from this roadside restaurant. A few years later, though—just when his life appeared on track—a new interstate was built and bypassed his town. The number of passersby plummeted, and his business tanked. He was forced to sell the property to pay his debts. Now 65 years old, after taking yet another lickin', Harland needed his $105-a-month Social Security checks just to get by.

But defeat wasn't on his agenda for long. With a stubborn smile, this white-haired, cane-supported man took his spices and pressure cooker and traveled the country marketing his recipe to restaurants. Harland saw potential in the restaurant franchising concept, and if a restaurant owner signed up with him, he received a nickel or so for each chicken they sold.

Incredibly, in the years ahead, his business matured from a one-man oper-ation into a flourishing global company. Today more than 40,000 KFC fast-food restaurants are in more than 50 countries around the world.

Harland was never too old, and it was never too late. Later in his life, and with a tale to tell behind every wrinkle, he was baptized in the Jordan River. Today, in the KFC museum at the headquarters for YUM! Brands, is a small, mostly unnoticed black-and-white photograph of Harland being baptized. (For more than a decade, this museum was near my office and in the same building.)

At the age of 90, he gave away most of his money. Though he didn't hit a home run right away, Colonel Harland David Sanders's original hard-knocks life story is a reminder that clarity in becoming what God intends is often a by-product of time and doing. When you drive by a KFC, be reminded of Har-land's story and God's faithfulness and perfect timing. You're never too old, and it's never too late. In time, God can use anyone to accomplish His purposes—sure, even someone wearing a black string tie and a stark white suit.

Now let me tell you a bit more about Daniel Nava. When he entered high school, he stood four feet eight inches and weighed less than 80 pounds and was considered too scrawny to excel in athletics. "After high school, failing to make the first college team he tried out for, Nava accepted the equipment manager's job and never complained. Undrafted out of college, he hired on with the Chico (California) Outlaws, a now-defunct independent minor league team that, at least initially, didn't want him either."[18]

Faced with rejection, he returned to his hometown, where he worked as a coach assistant without pay. "I basically thought I was done," recalls Nava. "If you don't get drafted or make an independent ball team, there's not much left."[19]

The next year, with a vacancy, the Outlaws called again. Nava made the most of this second chance and hit for a high average. Mildly (but hardly) impressed, the Red Sox paid the Outlaws a paltry one dollar for his contract rights.

After several subsequent years toiling in the minor league system, he was called to join the Boston Red Sox.

I told you what happened when he got there. Since his debut grand slam, he's continued his strong major league performance. Recently, he received the team's Lou Gorman Award. Named for the late general manager, the honor is given annually to a player who has "demonstrated dedication and perseverance in overcoming obstacles" on his way to the major league.

Nava, a heart-wired believer, reflected on his faith and God's mighty power during baseball's inevitable ups and downs: "I've found that in the craziness of this sport, of me going up and down, [faith has] been like a rock." With confidence, he shared, "I personally believe I'm here to do more than play baseball."[20]

When it comes to your early work choices, don't expect to hit a home run right away. Rather, as you've seen with Harland Sanders and Daniel Nava, prepare to be beautifully refined by your Creator in the years ahead. And as a believer, when faced with *I can't do it* obstacles in your workplace, with God as your co-laborer, do your best to—okay, I'll say it—never say Nava.

CHAPTER 6: TAKING STEPS FORWARD

A. Here's more from the Smithsonian account of Blondin's accomplishments: "By the time he gave his final performance in 1896, it was estimated that Blondin had crossed Niagara Falls 300 times and walked more than 10,000 miles on his rope. He died of complications from diabetes the following year. In nearly 73 years on this earth, he never had life insurance. No one, he'd always joked, would take the risk."[21]

B. Scripture is filled with the kind of "Oh no, not me!" call-response or approach-avoidance narrative. For some, I'm reminded of the intensity of a sobbing child being dropped off at preschool. In response to a call, Moses may have suffered tongue strain in shrieking, "Lord, please! Send anyone else" (Exodus 4:13 NLT). Also, we read in the book of Judges that when an angel of the Lord approached Gideon, the angel called him "mighty warrior." Gideon responded, "Mighty warrior? You've got the wrong guy!" In his eyes, he was neither "mighty" nor "warrior." Though Gideon was never a Special Forces soldier, God proceeded to use him in mighty and powerful ways.

C. Did you know that in direct speech, Jesus was addressed as "Teacher" more than 30 times in Scripture? The first year of His ministry is recapped in Matthew 9:35: "Jesus went through all the towns and villages, teaching in their synagogues, proclaiming the good news of the kingdom and healing every disease and sickness." And after His arrest, He said, "Am I leading a rebellion, that you have come out of with swords and clubs to capture me? Every day I sat in the temple courts teaching, and you did not arrest me" (Matthew 26:55).

At the end of the Sermon on the Mount, we're told, "The crowds were amazed at his teaching, because he taught as one who had authority, and not as their teachers of the law" (Matthew 7:28-29).

Interestingly, Jesus Christ referred to Himself as "Teacher" in Matthew 23:8-10. Is it any surprise, then, that the word *disciple* means "pupil" or "learner"?

CHAPTER 7: EMBRACING CHANGE

A. From Aesop's Fables, also known as the Aesopica, comes this story: One fine day in winter, some ants were busy drying their store of corn, which had become rather damp during a long spell of rain. Presently, up came a grasshopper, who begged them to spare her a few grains. "For," she said, "I'm simply starving."

The ants stopped work for a moment, though this was against their principles. "May we ask," said they, "what you were doing with yourself all last summer? Why didn't you collect a store of food for the winter?"

"The fact is," replied the grasshopper, "I was so busy singing that I hadn't the time."

"If you spent the summer singing," countered the ants, "you can't do better than spend the winter dancing." And they chuckled and went on with their work.

B. One week before he was assassinated, civil-rights leader Reverend Martin Luther King Jr. spoke the following words to thousands at the Washington National Cathedral: "Yes, we do live in a period where changes are taking place. And there is still the voice crying through the vista of time saying, 'Behold, I make all things new; former things are passed away.'" For more detail on this sermon, see Ben A. Franklins, "Dr. King Hints He'd Cancel March If Aid Is Offered," *New York Times*, April 1, 1968, and Nan Robertson, "Johnson Leads U.S. in Mourning: 4,000 Attend Service at Cathedral in Washington," *New York Times*, April 6, 1968.

CHAPTER 8: BEING WHOLEHEARTED

A. P.T. Barnum, a showman most remembered for his founding of the Barnum & Bailey Circus, fell gravely ill late in his storied life. At his request, a New York newspaper printed his obituary in advance so he could enjoy reading about his many accomplishments.[22]

With an entirely different emphasis, years ago Martin Luther encouraged us "to put our whole trust in his mercy and with utter certainty and without any doubt to have faith that we ourselves and all our works are pleasing to him not because of our worthiness or merit but because of his goodness."[23]

The so-called "good works" certainly have their place—not as part of an attempt to justify ourselves before God but as a response to having been justified by God through the work of Jesus.

With that in mind, consider this poem, which I've titled "Under Solomon's $un."

> I approached my labor with greediness; an address encased in glass. With some strains from stress of things to do, prideful assignments weathered fast. Urgent seasons and meaningless tasks, I can't remember. Don't ask. I chased the bearings to and fro, most times pursued for cash. Works' vapor in the wind, confess? Yes! Accept my thanks for verses past. Your wisdom scribed those years ago prioritizes that which lasts. O Lord, I know what's done for You alone shall be everlast.

B. Will we work in heaven? It's a heady question to consider! Though I don't speak from firsthand experience (yet), I can acquaint you with three perspectives: "We just don't know," "labor stoppage," and "service continued."

First, those replying that *we just don't know* shrug their shoulders and mention 1 Corinthians 2:9: "What no eye has seen, what no ear has heard, and what no human mind has conceived—the things God has prepared for those who love him." They maintain that in some mysterious fashion, your eternal service will take on a form and function we can only imagine and anticipate with hope.

Second, those embracing *labor stoppage* see earthly work as having no intrinsic value reference Revelation 21:2 (i.e., the "new" Jerusalem as "coming down out of heaven") and state that heaven contains no imperfection such as our gritty labor on earth (see 1 Corinthians 13:10, which says, "When the time of perfection comes, these partial things will become useless" (NLT).

And third, people believing *service continued* avow that some good and dirt-free portion of work will survive, be molded into eternal form, and contribute to the heavens forever. With this view, no matter if you're a politician, grave digger, or professional golfer, you get to see a preview of coming attractions now. The verses often cited are 1 Corinthians 15:58 ("Your labor in the Lord is not in vain") and Revelation 14:13 ("For their deeds will follow them").

To learn more, consider reading what Randy Alcorn penned in his book *Heaven* (Carol Stream, IL: Tyndale House, 2004) and reading Darrell Cosden's book *The Heavenly Good of Earthly Work* (Peabody, MA: Hendrickson, 2006).

As well, check out "Leaf by Niggle" by J.R.R. Tolkien. Tolkien, an English writer and university professor, is best known as the author of *The Hobbit, The Lord of the Rings*, and *The Silmarillion*. His short story "Leaf by Niggle" is often seen as an allegory of his creative process, and, to an extent, of his own life. In addition, it's an example of *service continued*, in which we continue some form (i.e., no longer flawed, destroyed, or incomplete) of our earthly work when in heaven. See J.R.R. Tolkien, *Tree and Leaf* (Washington, DC: Trinity Forum, 2003).

NOTES

ABOUT THIS BOOK

1. Ben Witherington III, *Work: A Kingdom Perspective on Labor* (Grand Rapids, MI: Wm. B. Eerdmans Publishing Co., 2011), viii.

2. Os Hillman, "Jesus Was a Workplace Minister," January 8, 2019, https://todaygodisfirst.com/jesus-was-a-workplace -minister.

3. D.H. Jensen, *Responsive Labor: A Theology of Work* (Louisville, KY: Westminster John Knox Press, 2006), 22.

CHAPTER 1: GOD CAN USE ANYONE

1. Lester DeKoster, *Work: The Meaning of Your Life—A Christian Perspective* (Grand Rapids, MI: Christian's Library Press, 2010), 5.

2. Cited in *One Hundred and One Famous Poems*, compiled by Roy J. Cook (Chicago, IL: Contemporary Books, Inc., 1958), 37.

3. Cited in John Dickson, *A Doubter's Guide to Jesus: An Introduction to the Man from Nazareth for Believers and Skeptics* (Grand Rapids, MI: Zondervan, 2018), 221.

CHAPTER 2: WORK IS *WORK*

1. Jeff Van Duzer, *Why Business Matters to God* (Downers Grove, IL: InterVarsity Press, 2010), 32.

2. *The Nicomachean Ethics* (New York, NY: Oxford University Press, 1925), 261.

3. For more details, see Hugh Whelchel, *How Then Should We Work?* (Bloomington, IN: WestBow Press, 2012), 13-20.

4. Ken Costa, *God at Work: Live Each Day with Purpose* (Nashville, TN: Thomas Nelson, 2016), 5.

5. Os Hillman, "Jesus Was a Workplace Minister," January 8, 2019, https://todaygodisfirst.com/jesus-was-a-workplace -minister.

CHAPTER 3: WHAT'S THE POINT?

1. David McCullough, *The Wright Brothers* (New York, NY: Simon & Schuster, 2015), 116.

2. John Calvin, *Institutes of the Christian Religion*, ed. John T. McNeill, trans. Ford Lewis Battles (Louisville, KY: Westminster Press, 1960), III.11.6.725.

3. https://www.beliefnet.com/quotes/evangelical/a/a-w-tozer/let-us-practice-the-fine-art-of-making-every-work .aspx.

4. Cited in *Always Look at the Bright Side*, compiled by Allen Klein (Berkeley, CA: Viva Editions, 2013), 176.

5. Abraham Kuyper, *Abraham Kuyper: A Centennial Reader*, ed. James D. Bratt (Grand Rapids, MI: Wm. B. Eerdmans Publishing Co., 1998), 461.

6. Annie Dillard, *Teaching a Stone to Talk: Expeditions and Encounters* (New York, NY: Harper & Rowe, 1982), 89.

7. "Lottery Winner Still Plowing Snow in Minnesota," Fox 9 News on KMSP-TV Minneapolis-St. Paul, Minnesota: November 11, 2014, https://www.youtube.com/watch?v=XytHt7ZdgIc.

CHAPTER 4: YOUR WHY

1. "Wonder On: Kelvyn Koning," https://youtu.be/okue_FgqSE8.

2. Katie Davis with Beth Clark, *Kisses from Katie: A Story of Relentless Love and Redemption* (New York, NY: Howard Books, 2011), 22.

3. Mother Teresa, as quoted in *No Greater Love*, ed. Becky Benenate and Joseph Durepos (New York, NY: MJF Books, 1997), 67.

4. Eusebius, as quoted in Leland Ryken, *Work and Leisure: In Christian Perspective* (Portland, OR: Multnomah, 1987), 66.

5. Eusebius, as quoted in Leland Ryken, *Work and Leisure*, 66. For a review of a Christian perspective on work and various influencers, see also Charles Colson and Nancy Pearcey, *How Now Shall We Live?* (Wheaton, IL: Tyndale House, 1999), 383-95.

6. James Martin, SJ, and Jeremy Langford, *Professions of Faith: Living and Working as a Catholic* (New York, NY: Sheed & Ward, 2002), xiii.

7. Martin Luther, *Werke Kritische Gesamtausgabe*, vol. 44 (Weimar, Germany: Hermann Bohlaus, 1883), 6.

8. Martin Luther, "The Estate of Marriage," in *Works*, vol. 45, ed. Walther I. Brandt (Philadelphia, PA: Fortress Press, 1962), 40.

9. A.W. Tozer, *The Pursuit of God* (Abbotsford, WI: Aneko Press, 2015), 110.

10. Charles Spurgeon, *Foretastes of the Heavenly Life* (1857), quoted in *Spurgeon's Expository Encyclopedia* (Grand Rapids, MI: Baker, 1951), 8:424.

11. Frederick Buechner, *Now and Then: A Memoir of Vocation* (Cambridge, MA: Harper & Row, 1983), 87.

12. Edward P. Hahnenberg, *Awakening Vocation: A Theology of Christian Call* (Collegeville, MI: Liturgical Press, 2010), 84.

13. Cited in Leland Ryken, *Work and Leisure*, 95, 97.

14. For more on Luther and the "priesthood of all believers" and work as vocation, see *Selected Writings of Martin Luther*, ed., Theodore G. Tappert (Minneapolis, MI: Fortress Press, 2007) and *Martin Luther, Three Treatises* (Fortress, 1970).

CHAPTER 5: SMART-WITH-HEART ACTIONS

1. Warren DeVos, as quoted in "Artist at Last," https://calvin.edu/publication/spark/2010/03/01/artist-at-last.

2. Prepared text of the commencement address delivered by Steve Jobs, CEO of Apple Computer and of Pixar Animation Studios, on June 12, 2005, https://news.stanford.edu/2005/06/14/jobs-061505/.

3. Malcolm Gladwell, *Outliers: The Story of Success* (New York, NY: Little, Brown, and Company, 2008), 39.

4. Thomas Alvin Boyd, *Charles F. Kettering* (Frederick, MD: Beard Books, 2002), 40.

5. Chip and Dan Heath, *Decisive: How to Make Better Choices in Life and Work* (New York, NY: Crown Publishing Group, 2013), 3.

6. Timothy Keller, "Christian Reflections on the Subject of Risk by Tim Keller," Ei Forum on Risk: Faith or Folly, April 5, 2013, https://www.youtube.com/watch?v=ki7w_29pYsg.

7. Tom Nelson, *Work Matters* (Wheaton, IL: Crossway Books, 2011), 88.

CHAPTER 6: TAKING STEPS FORWARD

1. Karen Abbott, "The Daredevil of Niagara Falls," Smithsonian.com, October 18, 2011, https://www.smithsonian mag.com/history/the-daredevil-of-niagara-falls-110492884/.

2. Kathleen K. Reardon, "Courage as a Skill," *Harvard Business Review*, January 2007, https://hbr.org/2007/01/courage-as-a-skill.

3. Adam Smith, *Wealth of Nations* (New York: Oxford University Press, 1981), I: 26-27.

4. Elisha Anderson, "Mummified woman was dead for 5 years and no one knew," *Detroit Free Press,* March 2, 2015, https://www.freep.com/story/news/local/2015/02/28/mystery-mummified-body-year-later/24188637/.

CHAPTER 7: EMBRACING CHANGE

1. Martin Ford, *Rise of the Robots: Technology and the Threat of a Jobless Future* (New York, NY: Basic Books, 2015), xiv.

2. Jerry Kaplan, *Humans Need Not Apply* (New Haven, CT: Yale University Press, 2015), 12-13.

3. McKinsey Global Institute, "Jobs Lost, Jobs Gained: Workforce Transitions in a Time of Automation," *Executive Summary*, December 2017.

4. Cathy N. Davidson, *The Future of Learning Institutions in a Digital Age: The John D. and Catherine T. MacArthur Foundation Reports on Digital Media and Learning* (Cambridge, MA: The MIT Press, 2009).

5. Virginia Heffernan, "Education Needs a Digital-Age Upgrade," *The New York Times*, Opinionator, August 7, 2011, https://opinionator.blogs.nytimes.com/2011/08/07/education-needs-a-digital-age-upgrade/.

6. Arnold Thackray, David Brock, and Rachel Jones, *Moore's Law: The Life of Gordon Moore, Silicon Valley's Quiet Revolutionary* (New York, NY: Basic Books, 2015), xx.

7. Ford, *Rise of the Robots*, xii-xiii.

8. Charles H. Spurgeon, *The Devotional Classics of C.H. Spurgeon: A Book of Daily Devotions containing Morning and Evening, I and II* (Lafayette, IN: Sovereign Grace Publishers Inc., 1990), Morning, November 2.

CHAPTER 8: BEING WHOLEHEARTED

1. Cited in Gustaf Wingren, *Luther on Vocation* (Minneapolis, MN: Fortress Press; rpt. Evansville, IN: Ballast Press, 1994), 33.

2. Jefferson Bethke, *It's Not What You Think: Why Christianity Is About So Much More Than Going to Heaven When You Die* (Nashville, TN: Thomas Nelson, 2015), 121.

3. Dorothy L. Sayers, *Creed or Chaos* (New York, NY: Harcourt Brace, 1949), 42-43.

4. John Van Sloten, *Every Job a Parable: What Walmart Greeters, Nurses, and Astronauts Tell Us about God* (Carol Stream, IL: NavPress, 2017), 6, 29.

5. Timothy Keller, *Every Good Endeavor: Connecting Your Work to God's Work* (New York, NY: Penguin Books, 2014), 63.

6. My short poem is a tip of the cap to "Christopher Robin Is Saying His Prayers" by A.A. Milne.

7. Isaiah 55:8-9.

WHAT'S MOST IMPORTANT TO YOU?

1. John Dickson, *A Doubter's Guide to Jesus: An Introduction to the Man from Nazareth for Believers and Skeptics* (Grand Rapids, MI: Zondervan, 2018), 221.

"WHAT IF I HATE WHAT I'M DOING?"

1. "Gallup Daily: U.S. Employee Engagement," https://news.gallup.com/poll/180404/gallup-daily-employee -engagement.aspx.

2. C.S. Lewis, *God in the Dock* (Grand Rapids, MI: Wm. B. Eerdmans, 1994), 52.

3. Helen Keller, *The World I Live In: A Collection of Essays* (Mineola, NY: Dover Publications, 2014), 91.

GOING DEEPER

1. William Morris, *Where Is God at Work?* (Oxford, England: Monarch Books, 2015), 222-23.

2. Jeff Van Duzer, *Why Business Matters to God* (Downers Grove, IL: InterVarsity Press, 2010), 19.

3. Ben Witherington III, *Work: A Kingdom Perspective on Labor* (Grand Rapids, MI: Wm. B. Eerdmans Publishing Co., 2011), 21.

4. A.W. Tozer, *The Pursuit of God* (Abbotsford, WI: Aneko Press, 2015), 103.

5. Tozer, *The Pursuit of God*, 110.

6. William Tyndale, *Doctrinal Treatises and Introductions to Different Portions of the Holy Scriptures*, ed. Henry Walter (Cambridge, England: The University Press, 1848), 102.

7. Gene Edward Veith Jr., *God at Work: Your Christian Vocation in All of Life* (Wheaton, IL: Crossway, 2011), back cover.

8. Veith, *God at Work*, 68.

9. Witherington, *Work*, 13.

10. Witherington, *Work*, 32.

11. Nikie Mayo, "Billy Graham's nephew, who lives in Anderson, is not mourning the loss of his uncle," *Anderson Independent Mail*, February 21, 2018, https://www.independentmail.com/story/news/2018/02/21/billy-grahams-nephew -shares-memories-man-he-knew/358730002/.

12. Gordon T. Smith, *Consider Your Calling: Six Questions for Discerning Your Vocation* (Downers Grove, IL: IVP Books, 2016), 38-40, 48.

13. Ken Costa, *God at Work: Living Each Day with Purpose* (Nashville, TN: Thomas Nelson, 2016), 39.

14. Lee Hardy, *The Fabric of This World: Inquiries into Calling, Career Choice, and the Design of Human Work* (Grand Rapids, MI: Wm. B. Eerdmans Publishing Co., 1990), 85.

15. Hardy, *The Fabric of This World*, 87.

16. "97-Year-Old Dies Unaware of Being Violin Prodigy," *The Onion*, https://local.theonion.com/97-year-old-dies-unaware-of-being-violin-prodigy-1819571799.

17. Douglas J. Schuurman, *Vocation: Discerning Our Vocations in Life* (Grand Rapids, MI: Eerdmans, 2004), chapter 2.

18. Joseph P. Kahn, "Daniel Nava, the long shot," *Boston Globe Magazine*, August 11, 2013, https://www.bostonglobe.com/magazine/2013/08/10/how-red-sox-outfielder-daniel-nava-overcame-odds/9bRXtsSLC9kxlY0OPsBs4O/story.html.

19. Kahn, "Daniel Nava, the long shot," *Boston Globe Magazine*.

20. Kahn, "Daniel Nava, the long shot," *Boston Globe Magazine*.

21. Karen Abbott, "The Daredevil of Niagara Falls," October 18, 2011, https://www.smithsonianmag.com/history/the-daredevil-of-niagara-falls-110492884.

22. Philip B. Kunhardt Jr., Philip B. Kunhardt III, and Peter W. Kunhardt, *P. T. Barnum: America's Greatest Showman* (New York, NY: Knopf, 1995).

23. Martin Luther, *Luther's Works*, vol. 26 (St. Louis, MO: Concordia, 1958), 277.

About the Author

Tom Heetderks has been a Human Resources leader for more than 30 years. He's worked at and consulted with some of the most well-known and successful organizations in the world.

For several years, Tom has served as vice president of Human Resources at ResCare. ResCare is the largest private provider of services to people with disabilities, the largest privately-owned home care company, the largest provider of specialized high-acuity neuro-rehab in community settings, and the largest career center workforce contractor in the US.

Earlier in his career, Tom was the executive sponsor for work on human capital initiatives with Kenexa/IBM's largest accounts, including companies such as Alcoa, Accenture, ExxonMobil, Macy's, and Glaxo SmithKline. And before that, for 15 years, Tom was a Human Resources executive with PepsiCo/YUM! Brands, helping to drive Human Resources processes across a global system of 35,000 restaurants and 1.4 million employees in more than 110 countries. YUM! Brands is the parent company for KFC, Pizza Hut, and Taco Bell.

Tom has a BA in Psychology and both an MA and Ph.D in Industrial/ Organizational Psychology. He is a devoted husband and the father of three grown children.

You can connect with Tom at
WorkWorthDoingTH@gmail.com.

To learn more about Harvest House books and
to read sample chapters, visit our website:

www.harvesthousepublishers.com

HARVEST HOUSE PUBLISHERS
EUGENE, OREGON